CW01430339

Published by:

FriesenPress
Suite 300 – 852 Fort Street
Victoria, BC, Canada V8W 1H8

www.friesenpress.com

Distributed to the trade by The Ingram Book Company

Foreword

In this volume, the third of the *Wanderings and Sojourns* series, favourite poems and songs from the two previous volumes are combined with many others that have not previously been published to form a collection that spans four decades of the author's itinerant life.

Touching, like its predecessors, on myriad themes this book is a collection of experiences and philosophies put to lyrical verse that were earned from a wanderer's existence embracing everything from war to love, ocean to forest, death to life, sorrow to humour with insight that delves into the heart of each subject, and at times even into the heart of the reader.

Whether a parody of a famous song, a mariner's tale, a story of a mythical creature, a lament for lost love, readers will be drawn to seek their own interpretations of what these words relate for them as the lines disturb slumbering memories and perhaps expose forgotten emotions of their own.

This book is dedicated to the many travelers who, upon wandering through their own life's journeys, have in their hearts their own poems and songs upon which to reflect and perhaps one day to share…

For we are of the fellowship, that scattered nomad clan
Who've walked life's trails with neither chart nor plan.
We went because we knew we should,
Wherever ways and times proved good.
We went because we could, as yet we can,
To see what life may show a wandering man.

Never Try to Cage the Wandering Breeze

Never try to cage the wandering breeze
That blows with scented breath from distant lands.
Never track its journey 'cross the seas
Which brought it to your open, searching hands.
Never ask how long it yet may stay
To cool the burning turmoil of your past,
Or gently warm the cold where memories play
On what was once a future that was destined not to last.

Harness, though, its strength beneath your wings
That you may fly to heights born of your dreams.
Hearken well the ancient words it sings
Explaining why life's not the way it seems.
Ride it to the lands that you desire
Where fate had always barred your younger road
By turning dreams into the raging fire
Which scorched the very footfalls where
your love and hope once strode.

Wonder at the places it has been
Though ask not that you know where it may go.
Study well the lessons it has seen
That you may understand what they may show.
Ask for just this instant to be shared
That always past and future may be free.
And never let your spirit once be scared
Should ever it depart to cross again that endless sea.

Hold it gently in your open hand.
Embrace its warmth. Caress its gentle smile.
Know that it will quietly understand
And satisfy your yearnings for a while.
Until the tides or seasons turn again,
And calls from distant lands are growing strong
To leave where it may long to yet remain,
To go where, like your open hands, it never will belong.

Never try to cage the wandering breeze
That blows with scented breath to distant lands.
Never track its journey 'cross the seas
Which takes it from your open, loving hands.
Never ask how long it may be gone
Or where its wayward journey may be cast.
Walk the road it's love placed you upon,
For there will lie you future that is destined now to last.

Never try to cage the wandering breeze,
Nor track its endless journey 'cross the freedom of the seas.
Never try to close your open hands,
For then it may return to you as destiny commands.

JIM SCOTT

Wanderings and Sojourns

THE SONGS AND VERSES

A Book of Poetry, Songs and Insight From a Wanderer's Life

3

Table of Contents

Definition of "*Wander*"
(Verb) **move about aimlessly or without any destination**

Definition of "*Sojourn*"
(Noun) **a temporary stay**

Dark Caribbean Rum

You can talk of the finest Clarets,
or the best of the Cotes du Rhone,
Sing praise to the vines that produce the great wines
Such as Burgundy, Bordeaux or Beaune.
When all's said and done there is only the one
That counts when the evening has come
With need to unwind and relax the old mind
… That's dark Caribbean rum.

There's merit in most of the scotches,
and vodka is well worth a try.
And no need to pass if you're offered a glass
Graced with gin or with bourbon or rye.
But when someone asks for what's best from the casks
And says they would like to have some,
It's better than not that you pour them a tot
… Of dark Caribbean rum.

And lager is grand at a party, and stout is quite pleasant to down.
Of all the fine brews there's some good ones to choose
In a bitter or pale ale or brown.
But should you need think of a versatile drink
Enjoyed both in mansion and slum,
There's really no doubt what you're thinking about,
… It's dark Caribbean rum.

So as you try all that's been brewing, and
sample whatever's distilled,
Put each to test so you'll know what is best
For your palate to always be thrilled;
And tried every brand brought from every land
'Till your mind and your taste buds are numb,
You'll honour your thirst with the one that came first
… That's dark Caribbean rum.
So pour from the flask if you're up to the task
In measures the width of your thumb,
And don't try to hog all that glorious grog,
But let's share a toast to the one we love most
… The dark Caribbean rum!

"A man should never be ashamed to own he has been in the wrong, which is but saying, in other words, that he is wiser today than he was yesterday."
... Alexander Pope

Unforgiven

There's no way I'll forgive you all the suffering I've felt
That brought me all those anguished tears I'd weep.
There's no exoneration for the ache my heart was dealt
That caused these lonely days,
those desperate nights devoid of sleep.
Nor any absolution for this sadness still inside
Nor for the utter agony I've known.
For why should I forgive you for the way our loving died,
When all the blame that must be borne is mine, and mine alone?

For you were not responsible for any wrongful deed
Beyond the gift of being a loving friend.
You gave to me your beauty and I paid you with my need,
Requiring far more energy than anyone should spend.
So how can I accuse you for the times we two have shared?
…That you showed me a better way to live?
…That you had loved so tenderly, and genuinely cared?
…That you received far less than all the gifts that you would give?

Of what could you be guilty then for which you might atone?
…For gently trying to slow my racing heart?
…For teaching me the many magic roads that you have shown?
…For showing how my past might end,
and future now might start?
No. There can be no accusation. There can be no blame.
There's nothing to forgive or to forget.
For you were never guilty. It is I who bears the shame
For how our loving friendship has so tragically been set.

So how can I forgive you for an uncommitted crime,
Which generates no need to reprehend.
Nor can I beg forgiveness, but I'll ask of you for time
To find where I again may earn the right to be your friend.
And I will ever thank you for the lessons I have learned
That influence how now I choose to live,
And help me reach that time when I have genuinely earned
The right to look back to the fool I was, and to forgive.

"To be able to look back upon one's life in satisfaction is to live twice."
...Kahlil Gibran

Sailors Farewell

So, now your tide is come on which to leave and set your sail.
Good luck my friend, I pray your journey's blessed.
My tides are done. My journey's past.
My winds can now but fail,
So beg of you I must this last request.

Should you voyage south to climes of sea, and sun and wine,
And meet there beauty shining, bronzed and tall,
Ask if she remembers when her plans would meld with mine.
Tell her that I did achieve them all.

But tell her not of the life I've led
Since I left her gentle shore.
Or the times my wandering heart has bled
For the maids I've loved before
That I will see no more.

Should you voyage east to where the rivers gently flow
Through rolling hills of forest, field and farm,
And meet perfection such that every mortal man should know,
Tell her that I did not come to harm.

But tell her not of the life I've led
Since the last she saw me go.
Or the times my wandering heart has bled
For the warmth that love can show
That never more I'll know.

Should you voyage west away to islands in the breeze
Where life is warm and days are slow to turn,
And meet there brown eyed wonder gazing long across the seas.
Tell her I have nothing left to learn.

But tell her not of the life I've led
Since she watched me sail away.
Or the times my wandering heart has bled
For the words we spoke that day
That never more I'll say.

Should you voyage north to lands of ice and fur and storm,
Where night becomes as endless as the cold,
And meet there glowing loveliness, both passionate and warm.
Tell her that I have not grown old.

But tell her not of the life I've led
Since I sailed out with the tide.
Or the times my wandering heart has bled
Or the tears I've often cried
I'll no more need to hide.

Then should you voyage back to where
you now cast off your line,
Remember the requests which I just gave.
And tell to me the stories of the memories which were mine.
Tell them to the headstone of my grave.

"Men go back to the mountains, as they go back to sailing ships at sea, because in the mountains and on the sea they must face up"
    ...Henry David Thoreau

Tomorrow's Past Life

There was once a time when my life was filled with living;
Adventure and excitement scattered all across this earth.
I was in my prime, with so much just ripe for giving.
To wander seemed the reason for my birth.
But now my life has changed, I seldom travel fifty mile.
Adventure's turned to mortgage. Mine's a sedentary style.
My freedom's now an office, distant romance an ex-wife.
I have to find the path that leads me on to my old life

So that just once more I can sail the endless ocean,
Or track the old bull wildebeest, and dive amongst the whales.
Watch the condors soar. Change my plans on any notion
To seek of lands heard in a stranger's tales.
Is that so very much to ask? I've known it so before.
The hunger and the plenty, forest snow and desert shore.
The laughter and the loneliness, the passions and the pain.
But still there's lands I didn't see, and those I'd see again

If I found a way to undo these chains that bind me,
Not harming those I love nor running from the debts I owe.
I should leave today! Going where no one could find me,
Not caring what I'd seek or where I'd go.
But that's now how my dreams are made; awake I see the truth:
The bank, the schools the eight to five, so absent from my youth,
Now plot against my wanderlust, my yearning for the road
To hide the path I'm seeking that I once so freely strode.

But there'll come a time when the house is bought and paid for,
The kid's are all through college and the pension's guaranteed.
Then I'll start to climb back toward the life I'm made for;
My chains released, my spirit once more freed.
Though twenty years may lie between this moment and that day,
It waits on the horizon as a cairn which points the way.
A monument to travelers; emancipation's prize!
A mark to set my compass bearing steady in my eyes
So that I can see that my life is far from finished.
And some day I will live again adventures yet untold.
Where the wind and me, with a passion undiminished,
Will find that younger life I knew of old.

Waking, and then Finding You Were There

Waking, and then finding you were there,
I gazed upon your smile and gently stroked your morning hair.
Wondering what brought us to that day.
Amazed we were together and you'd asked that I would stay.
For I was not the man who should have lain down at your side,
With shattered dreams, and dying hope,
and nowhere left to hide.
You took my hand and placed it on your heart
And showed me that my life had yet to start.

A person such as you should claim
A man with wealth and fame with whom to be...
...Yet you had chosen me!

Silently you led me from my pain,
And raised my spirit up 'till I began to hope again.
Tenderly my soul was bound with peace.
The torments of my past, my disillusions, found release.
For you brought more than loving to share with me that night;
Your soul was surely angel born, your spirit forged of light.
You kissed away the loneliness and fears,
And gently dried my eyes of ancient tears.

Just when I thought my love was killed
You started to rebuild my broken heart…
…And joined with yours each part.

And though a thousand miles now lie between
The place where I must wake alone,
and where we two have been.
I still can see the loving in your eyes
And hear your gentle laughter float across the morning skies.
For I am still there with you in more than just my dreams,
We've half each others heart inside us,
joined by silken seams.
Our souls still run united through the dawn
To where our single future life was born.

Though distance now between us lies
Your smile still fills my eyes as though you're here…
…I feel that you are near.

And even though our longing arms can't hold
The other to our heart with tender passion yet untold,
Our spirits intertwine all through the night.
Meeting in the silent stars that glow with burning light.
For we have shared the wonder that no one can explain
Which took my shattered life and made it hale and whole again,
And let my lonely broken heart revive,
And gave my love a reason to survive.

For we have shared the wonder that cannot be explained
Of love that knows no distance and that cannot be contained.
However far apart our hearts may be
I still can feel yours here inside of me.

"Love is a game in which one always cheats."
... Honoré de Balzac

His Secret Mistress

This is a tale of an immoral male
With a love that he keeps on the side.
Who at every chance will exploit that romance
That he hasn't a choice but to hide.
His wife of twelve years always fills him with fears
For there's no way that she understands it.
So he tells her his lies and then goes to his prize
Every time that his lover demands it.

He knows she'll be there quietly waiting just where
He had kissed her goodbye the last time.
The thought of that place brings a smile to his face
As he savours his secretive past time
When he goes to great pains with his shackles and chains
And his ropes and his bindings and lashings.
Though he knows it's all wrong, the excitement is strong
When releasing those deep hidden passions.

While he loves well his wife, he's this other half life
That he craves every day that he's waking.
And he knows it's not right when the money is tight
To be splitting the wages he's making.
But his lover's not cheap if he needs her to keep
Looking good like he wants when he sees her.
So he scrimps and he saves for the one that he craves,
And he hopes that his purchases please her.

But when they're alone, just the two on their own,
He knows that her worth can't be measured.
He hasn't a care what it cost to be there
When he's being so royally pleasured.
She's curvy and fast, built for fun that can last,
And she gives him the joys that he yearns for.
And she treats him so well that he always can tell
That he'll get what he always returns for.

Yet he knows in his heart that when they're apart
One fine day he will have to stop lying.
And his wife will find out just what he's been about
With the life on the side he's been trying.
And what'll he do when he finally comes true
That those evenings weren't spent down the pub?
But were all spent afloat on that thirty foot boat
That he keeps at the local yacht club.

"The future is something which everyone reaches at the rate of sixty minutes an hour, whatever he does, whoever he is."

...C.S. Lewis

The Choice that was Yesterday's

On to the dawn of tomorrow, and on
To the days that will turn into weeks.
And the weeks into months into years will be gone
'Till the choice that was yesterday's quietly speaks
To the dawn that its destiny seeks.

"What would life be if we had no courageto attempt anything?"
...Vincent Van Gogh

Life Well Lived

He's traveled every ocean where he charted every isle,
And rode out every storm there was to ride.
He mapped each un-trod valley as he claimed each verdant mile,
And thrived where other men had quietly given up and died.
He watched the ramparts crumble 'neath the blows of his attack
And raised the golden harvests from his fields.
But now he's grown older, and his path can't lead him back
Where once he walked amid the mists his memory now yields.

He earned a dozen fortunes, then he squandered every one,
Though treating each as brothers; dearth and feast.
He loved some wondrous women
'ere his loving years were done,
And judged not one was any more the greater or the least.
He lived life even handed and took everything in stride
And never moaned or bragged or wanted more…
…'Till now…
… as here he stands amid that final ebbing tide
That can but wash him lifeless 'pon that lonely western shore.

But even while his history comes blurred within his mind,
With much he once achieved beyond his sight,
He yet sees more than most, should they decide to look behind,
And knows the paths he chose, though
mostly challenging, were right.
He also knows he's filled his life with everything he could,
And gave more than he took along the way.
So…ancient now, and wise, he lets life choose the path it would,
And rests his eyes…
…and smiles…
…and lets the tide bear him away.

"In the depth of winter, I finally learned that there was within me an invincible summer."
... Albert Camus

Thaw

The snow has almost melted with the coming of the spring,
Except for where the sun can't penetrate
The shadows that remain throughout these still quite chilly days
And frosty nights. Where memory still sadly turns and plays
With thoughts of what once was, that congregate
About the optimism that the changing seasons bring.

The earth is now much softer as the ice begins to thaw
That once was cast as iron, hard and bleak.
Where dormant lay the seeds until the vernal summons cries,
Just like these seeds of love sewn 'neath
the gentle summer skies,
With hope they'd grow to be the dreams I seek.
To be but cruelly frozen by the one I'd see no more.

The icicles have gone now from beyond the windowpane,
Where through this longest winter they would stand
As bars about the prison where my captured spirit dwelt
Convicted of the loneliness and loss it then had felt
From witnessing the death of all we'd planned.
But now the ice has melted and my spirit's freed again.

And soon once more unfurling leaves and bursting buds I'll see,
And feel the warming breeze upon my skin,
And know the seasons turning will perennially give
New hope to fill my heart, and yet another love to live.
Another summer romance to begin
With little thought of autumns gone, or winters yet to be.
With little thought of anything, save her, and love, and me,
Rejuvenated by the thaw that casts our memories free.

"Vitality shows in not only the ability to persist but the ability to start over."
    ...F. Scott Fitzgerald

Hurricane Tree

Can't forget that night I watched you falling.
Biggest storm that summer sent our way.
Didn't think that you'd survive, nor let alone you'd be alive
To hear these words that now I need to say.
Just like you, my losses were appalling,
Everything I owned to wind and flood.
Laid my head down at your side. Can't recall how long I cried
Into that empty aftermath and mud.

You and I had both grown here together.
Day that I was born you too were small.
Both of us just grew and grew until I stood at forty two
As broad as you, though nowhere near as tall.
That was when we faced that fearsome weather,
When nature brought us both down to the ground.
Many folks since then have gone, but you and I just carried on,
With every little piece of hope we found.

Guess your tap-root held, though strained and hurting.
Just the same, my heart and soul survived.
You lay broken on your side and though
it seemed as you had died
From deep within your spirit was revived.
When I saw your first green buds start spurting,
Then I knew we both could make it through.
With every flower and every leaf, I put aside another grief
And started to create my life anew.

Through all my years you'd been my inspiration.
And even when you fell you didn't fail.
Holding on to tiny dreams you clung to life, and now it seems
Though crippled, you are strong of heart, and hale.
So watch me as I dig this new foundation,
Casting out what's past to build again.
Scarred from what that storm has cost,
but no more tears for what was lost,
Like you I have the future to sustain.

So here's to you for teaching me endurance
With all but hope destroyed before my eyes.
Your example turned the tide
and helped regain my shattered pride
And helped my broken spirit once more rise.
Only your strength gave that reassurance
Lending me the will to grow once more.
You and I, once near the end, now face
the future, friend and friend
To climb back to the lives we shared before.

"A good traveler has no fixed plans and is not intent on arriving."
...Lao Tzu

Travelers Upon the Road

We've traveled far from distant lands
and met here on these shores.
I've long forgotten many roads and know not much of yours.
But now we stand together as we face the same two doors
And neither of us knows the one to choose.
For one may lead me onward to a place I need to see.
For you it may be heading back to where you used to be.
The other may go nowhere, or it may yet need a key
We don't know where to find or how to use.

But if we take the same door will you travel on beside me,
Or wait until we cross the sill and go your way alone?
Or will you choose the other door, your company denied me,
To find your future travels on your own?

We've time before we need to pick the way we each should go,
So let us rest our weary legs and let our stories flow
About the ways we've wandered and the people that we know,
And share, but for a while, our vagrant years.
For I have had adventures, and I've felt my share of pain,
And you look like a vagabond with legends to explain.
We might as well share tales for we may never meet again,
And maybe there'll be no one else who hears.

So tell me of the life you've lived in all its sordid glory,
And I will tell to you so well, of mine with all its cost.
So when we wander on again we'll bear each other's story
That neither one should ever have been lost.

I've wandered since my birth
through trials and deeds beyond recall
And never knew the way to go or what fate might befall.
Through times when I could gallop or in times I had to crawl
The road I chose was that which carried on.
And what of you bold fellow in your tatters and your rags?
Like me you bear your past within
those patched and empty bags.
Were ever your paths clear or mostly overgrown with snags?
Describe for me the trails you've walked upon.

For you're my brother of the road that no one yet may tether.
You've come so far to where we are by means no one can trace.
You've wandered through a hundred lands
in every kind of weather,
Which carved the scars of struggle on your face.

And now we're done with resting we must face the road ahead,
I thank you for your stories and the words which you have said.
Now walk toward the door you choose,
and mind the paths you tread,
And guard with care the memories you hold.
For me, I'll take the other door, no matter where it leads.
Our paths were only meant to cross,
our lives have different needs.
Good luck in where you travel and be true in all your deeds,
And pray we'll meet again before we're old.

For we are just two travelers who met upon life's highway,
Like everyone since time begun, in every place you'll see.
And you must live the life you choose,
while I must do so my way,
And everyone's the same like you and me.

For everyone is different too, with different destinations.
All travel far from where they are to where they're going to go.
And when their paths may cross they'll stop
and share their conversations,
And tell of where they've been and what they know.
But always ever on they're bound to go.
Like you and I they're always bound to go.

"The wonder is always new that any sane man can be a sailor"
   ...Ralph Waldo Emerson

I am the Skipper

(To the tune of "I am the Walrus")

She and me upon the sea
When you and he, and we are altogether.
See how we sail like birds in a gale
See how we fly.
We're flying.
Sitting in the cockpit;
Waiting for the drinks to come.
Martin had to go to fetch the beer below
But Sally's been a naughty girl, she left them on the dock.
I am the yachtsman.
They are the yachtsmen.
I am the skipper
Go get the beer.

Listen mister silly sister
Sally left the beers behind again.
How can we cruise without any booze?
See how we try.
We're trying.
Sitting in the cockpit;
Wondering what we gonna do.
Martin with a frown said turn the boat around
'Cos Sally's been a naughty girl, she left the beer behind.
I am the yachtsman.
They are the yachtsmen.
I am the skipper.
Go get the beer.

Sitting on a drifting sail boat waiting for a drink.
If there is no beer…
I'm gonna have to steer the boat back to the club again!
I am the yachtsman.
They are the yachtsmen.
I am the skipper.
Go get the beer…Go get the beer
Go get the beer…Go get the beer

Yelling, huffing, gybing luffing,
No sense toughing out this situation.
How can we sail without any ale?
See how we cry.
We're crying.
Sitting in the cockpit,
Turning the ignition key.
Martin on the deck yelled "Crikey, what the heck!"
'Cos Sally's been a naughty girl and let the sails come down.
I am the yachtsman.
They are the yachtsmen.
I am the skipper.
Go get the beer...Go get the beer
Go get the beer...Go get the beer

With apologies and respect to Mr. Lennon and Mr. McCartney.
But I couldn't resist!

"On the ragged edge of the world I'll roam, and the home of the wolf shall be my home."
  ... Robert Service

Spirit Guide

Watching from the edge of vision,
Understanding all that moves,
Every step your silent mission
Universal wisdom proves.

Held within such savage beauty
Coiled to strike, or play, at will.
Sentinel, by choice and duty,
Ready there to die, or kill.

Ever feeling, ever flowing,
Cosmic synergies released.
Through man's darkest midnight glowing.
Primal spirit. Noble beast.

Watching o'er our misspent choices
Spirit Guide of ancient realm,
Show us by your mystic voices
Lest our darkness overwhelm.

Somewhere In Your Hidden Past

Somewhere in your hidden past there lies
An agony that haunts you to this day,
Which deep within your memory denies
Your heart to feel the freedom that can let love lead the way.

Sometime in your life there has been pain
Now buried someplace deep where you can't feel,
That manifests itself time and again,
Protecting you with memories from all love might reveal.

Taking all the warmth you feel inside,
It placed instead a cold defensive shield
That blocked the paths of tears you should have cried
To free you from the suffering those lonely memories yield.

There about that blockage lies the key
To let your passions rise to heights above,
And set your yearning spirit once more free,
To capture the excitement and ability to love.

Would that I could crawl inside your mind
To search within the darkness of before,
In hopes that I could gently try to find
And clear the 'prisoned feelings that so long you've held in store.

Would that I could free your lonely heart
To fly on questing wings to new found lands.
And be there as the dawn of love would start,
To feel awakened fervor in your eager open hands.

But sadly in your hidden past still lies
That agony that bars an honest friend,
And yet, despite your loneliness, denies
His quest to let your damaged heart once more begin to mend.

"Experience is the name everyone gives to their mistakes."
...Oscar Wilde

Wrecked

He's dreaming of the shore that he knows he'll see no more
And lamenting now his fate so cruelly tossed.
He never thought that life could go so fast,
The shadows of the past
are merely all the ghosts of what he's lost.
He used to run so free when he sailed upon the sea
Never knowing of the ports to which he'd call.
Adventure borne on every southern gale
Which filled his vagrant sail to take him every place and see it all.

And love he surely knew, whether false or whether true,
From as many girls as he'd seen distant lands.
But now his eyes look back toward the truth,
So hidden in his youth, and tears flow as he quietly understands.
He chose to sail alone, now he's stranded on his own
With no other soul with whom he might grow old.
He should have settled down and made a home,
But chose instead to roam
in search of what adventure's path might hold.

His journeys ended here where the waters run so clear,
And tomorrow's been decided by the past.
He didn't feel the turning of the tide,
Nor knew the sea might hide
the dangers where his future's now been cast.
He's grounded high and dry, as the ebbing tide flows by,
In a distant land he'd tried so hard to find.
He wished now that he chose the other tack
That would have sailed him back
to places he now yearns for in his mind.

His keel's been broke in two. He's no strength to build anew
And he hasn't got the spirit, nor the heart.
He's only got the memory of what's gone.
He wants to carry on, but doesn't see at his age how to start.
If only he'd have known of the pains from being alone
When the wind drove him upon this leeward shore,
He never would have set that wayward track
That never took him back
to where he thought of settling down before.

And dreaming of that isle brings a melancholy smile
As he thinks of all the happiness he lost.
That lass he'd left there waving from the sand
With flowers in her hand.
This empty soul his wanderlust has cost.
He turns to let the spray wash his bitter tears away
As he curses loud the calling of the sea.
His fists are clenched in anger at the thought
Of life so come to naught.
Of prison made from striving to be free.

He stares upon the waves and imagines there the graves
Of his fellow sailors similarly cast.
He puts another bottle to his lips
And while he quietly sips,
the present seems to blur into the past.
And once the bottle's drained he has youth and heart regained
And forgotten all the sadness of before.
He's running free again before the breeze
And challenging the seas
to carry him away from memory's shore.

While stumbling to stand with the bottle in his hand
He is hoisting every sail his dreams can find.
He sees the dolphins phosphorescent trail
Beside the leeward rail. The alcohol, this time is being kind.
And sailing to the shore that he'll never see once more
He is laughing at his fate so strangely tossed.
Reality could never live this fast,
Through shadows of the past,
and wasted opportunities now lost.

His mind is running free as it sails the open sea
Never knowing of the ports to which he'll call.
A memory on every southern gale
Which filled his younger sail,
to take him every place and see it all.
…A memory on every southern gale
…But now those winds must fail
…There's no more dreams to sail
…He's dreamed them all.

"Self defense is Nature's oldest law."
...John Dryden

Standard Issue Rifle

Night had settled quiet round the yawning ridge backed dogs.
The gates were locked. The reading chair pulled near
To where the rifle rested in the shadow of the logs.
There should uninvited guests appear.
No bullet in the barrel,
The safety catch was on.
Relaxed we sat and warmed before the flame.
No bullet in the barrel,
It's menace all but gone,
Its company gave comfort just the same.

Hours before we'd made a kill, though neither'd gone for sport,
We'd dropped a charging sable neatly dead.
Cornered there and gut shot bad, he couldn't run, so fought.
The hunter's gun had jammed, or so he said.
We weren't there for the hunting
But needed just in case
The terrorists should think to make a play.
We weren't there for the hunting
But hunters learned their place
As merciful, my rifle had its say.

It came from many miles away to help me in the wars.
He'd sneaked behind the backs of those in wait.
And crossed a dozen borders closed,
and through forbidden doors,
And busted every sanction, not too late.
I'd camouflaged his woodwork
And I'd camouflaged his steel.
And even camouflaged his magazine.
I'd camouflaged his woodwork
But I couldn't hide the feel
Of latent strength, now dormant; stern, not mean.

Then, while I traced his history, the dogs began to bark.
I killed the household lights and hit the floor.
I can't remember grabbing him, but hidden by the dark
Stealthily we both moved to the door.
The safety catch was off now,
A bullet in the breach.
The belt of magazines was slung behind.
The safety catch was off now,
Maybe danger within reach.
His heartless steel had cooled my boiling mind.

And then I saw the danger stand, but didn't squeeze a shot.
It could have made no difference to the war.
The dogs had sniffed a kudu at a nighttime feeding spot,
Where Jeb, the stable lad, had stored some straw.
There wasn't any danger,
But one of us had scared,
Though feeling somewhat foolish in the end.
There wasn't any danger,
But such adventure shared.
Can only serve to make a gun a friend.

For if he hadn't lived with me I doubt I could have slept.
Nor walked alone or worked about the farm.
I'd move away, for he alone is all that quietly kept
Me feeling safe from terroristic harm.
He's just an issued riffle
Like twenty thousand more
The government distributes every year.
He's just an issued riffle,
A soldier in a war.
But one who never knows the taste of fear.
He's just an issued riffle
Whose thanks are sparse and poor
For one that guarantees I still have breath!
Not just an issued riffle,
He's peace. He's upheld law.
A means of living. Not a source of death.

"I only feel angry when I see waste. When I see people throwing away things we could use."
   ...Mother Teresa

The Garage Sale

(To the tune of "Impossible Dream" from Man of La Mancha.)

To dream the impossible dream
To find the affordable seat.
Recline in unbearable comfort.
To take all this weight off my feet

To slouch on an overstuffed couch
And sink in its soft yielding foam,
And snooze when my eyes are too weary
To dream of a well furnished home.

This is my quest
To furnish my home
No matter how ancient
Or how far to roam.
I'll drive to your yard
Without question or pause
To be willing to load
Up my van with whatever was yours.

And I know if I'll only be true
To this furniture quest,
That my back will be thankful to you
When it lays down to rest.

And my kids will be grateful for this
That their dad, stiff and covered with fluff
Still drove with his last ounce of petrol
To reach all that second hand stuff.

To have matching tables and chairs,
A rack where to hang a clean shirt.
A mat where to make people welcome.
And rugs under which to sweep dirt.

And shelves onto which to place books
To look better read than I are.
A desk, so I might seem efficient.
A "drobe" with a prefix of war.

This is my quest,
To furnish my pad
With stuff I've long needed
But never have had.
And I'm willing to take
What you're willing to give.
And I'm willing to show
It new life in the place where I live

And I know that I cannot repay
Such a wonderful deed,
'Till that day when the 6/49
Puts an end to my need

And my house will resemble no more
The bare Spartan cell of a monk,
Because you, in the back of your garage,
Could reach all that obsolete junk.

"The judgment is in the hands of the True Guru, who puts an end to the argument. Whatever the Creator does, comes to pass. It cannot be changed by anyone's efforts."
...Sri Guru Granth Sahib

Judgment of Life

Times there are for each to try to manifest our reason.
Times when we might justify the purpose of our birth.
All may have a moment, or a day, or yet a season,
Crediting our presence and our legacy on earth.

Chance there'll be to rectify the burden of our living.
Chance to try to mitigate the weight of being born.
Arbitrated so by every judgment unforgiving
Universal courts decree with pleasure, or with scorn.

Such may be the times unprecedented evil finds you.
Such may be the deeds performed when challenges are met.
So shall be the evidence by which life's judgment binds you,
Instant in its verdict, though eternal to forget.

Rise to these occasions then to honour well your duty.
Rise to every challenge borne afresh at each new day.
Fight each unearthed ugliness with unrelenting beauty.
Wield the blade of honesty, though mind well what you slay.

Guard the unprotected 'neath the shelter of your shield.
Guard all universal truths that others have depraved.
Seed the crops of tolerance in hatred's barren field.
Rescue captives from despair, yet know not whom you saved.

Strive to bear the flag of hope for all who may be falling.
Strive to heal the wounded so they yet may rise again.
Stand to every unjust foe, and hold fast to your calling.
Seek the light of guidance, and care nothing for your pain.

Spread the glow of love within the battles darkest hours.
Spread the goal of peace amid the fiercest of the fray.
Know that if your fight be just the universal powers
Stand beside you, rank on rank, to help you win the day.

Honour then the vanquished,
help them heal and stand beside you.
Honour too their future and their place beneath the sun.
Go then back from where the universe had found and tried you.
Dwell not on the victory, nor count what has been won.

Ask not recognition. Neither gratitude nor glory.
Ask not of the Arbitrator's knowledge of your cause.
Face the mediocrity he casts about your story.
Seek not his affection and expect not his applause.

Never try to change his arbitration once it's stated.
You may only influence before that judgment's made.
Deeds performed and finished, not desires contemplated,
Counsel his tribunal on the contribution paid.

Live well then each moment, every day of every season.
Live with deeds of charity, commitment and of trust.
Think not of your value, only scrutinize your reason.
Worth is judged by life itself. Impartially, and just.

"Voyaging belongs to seamen, and to the wanderers of the world who cannot, or will not, fit in."
...Sterling Hayden

Tavern Not Far From The Shore

Between the sea and coming ashore
In tidal zones of emotion,
Washed by ebbs of the cottage door
And floods of the open ocean,
Amphibious beings restlessly stand
In the lee of their wind-swept past,
Talking of days when the sea had command
And years they spent under the mast.
And some may be wandering seaward,
While others to land may be bound.
And some never know of the way they should go
So wash up wherever they're found.
And some folk may never stop sailing,
While others may sail no more.
But all find their way at the close of the day
To the tavern, not far from the shore.

"Still this planet's soil for noble deeds grants scope abounding."
   ...Johann Wolfgang von Goethe

More Noble Than The dawn

Leave now each day more noble than its start
That dusk might tell the morrow's dawn your way,
Of how you walked so guided by your unrequiring heart,
And how you should be granted one more day.

Look to each morn, and how you'd then begun
To honour well this realm through which you came.
Ask if you gave more than took in all that you have done,
And treated every yesterday the same.

Ask not the dusk if you have earned your place
Among those granted breath upon the morrow's first grey light.
But search instead your footprints
that your conscience well should trace,
And contemplate the judgment of the night.

Answer yourself, if you deserve the morn
That comes to those who leave each day
more noble than the start.
For you alone determine how your sun shall be reborn
By paths you took to where it did depart.
And you alone determine how your sun shall be reborn
By making sure each sunset is more noble than the dawn.

"A man's real life is that accorded to him in the thoughts of other men by reason of respect or natural love."
...Joseph Conrad

The Mate

I've rarely seen a man who could have stood his ground so long
No matter what the odds or where the fight.
I've never seen another who could prove he wasn't wrong
When every one could prove he wasn't right.
I've sailed with many bastards but I've never met the man
Whose discipline was harder than the one this fellow gave.
Yet I've seen no other person, from Helsinki to Saipan,
Whose tolerance was greater, or whose justice was so brave.

We respected him for the strengths that he would show
Which kept us on an even keel and made a mob a crew.
Yet we loathed him too for the lengths that he would go
To make sure we had loads of work to do.

There wasn't any one of us could say we didn't owe
At least a debt of gratitude or two.
For some it was hard money,
but there's no one else would know,
He never told a soul of what he'd do.
And I think there's not a one of us he hasn't carried back
From drinking way too much in places we should not have been.
Yet all of us he's threatened with deductions, or the sack.
He can be a saint or demon, or whatever in between.

And there's times I've known when all of us could kill
The bastard that's been working each beyond his mortal bound.
Then there's storms we've shared when just his stubborn will
Was all that bought us homeward hale and sound.

So when each hell-sent trip is done and all the lads ashore
Are supping up a pint to say good-bye.
We, every single one of us, say we'll be back no more
We'll give another livelihood a try.
Yet when the leave is all but up with money getting low
We wander back to where we said we wouldn't go again,
And sign back on the same old line, as if we didn't know
The hardships we was choosing, all the toil, the fights, the pain.

And the reason why it happens every trip
That brings us back to face the life we know we're going to hate?
It's not the pay, the company, nor the ship.
It's that bastard that we all respect: The Mate.

"The sea, once it casts its spell, holds one in its net of wonder forever."
   ...Jacques-Yves Cousteau

A Sailor's Rivals

Me Dad was workin' with the sea from nineteen thirty four.
'E died when I was just turned three. Torpedoed in the war.
I can't say's I remember ought. Me Mam still says she can
She keep's 'is photos lyin' about: "Our Jenny, love from Dan."

I think 'e only saw me twice before 'e went below.
'Is death come as an 'eavy price to a son 'e'd never know.
But if e'd still been livin' on an' sailing all 'is life.
'E'd not 'ave known 'is only son. Nor would 'e know 'is wife.

An' still today the life's the same for those with kids, at sea.
Me nipper said when last I came 'e don't remember me!
Me daughter, just turned seven now, a smashin' little piece,
She acts around me more like 'ow she would were she my niece.

The wife, she's like their Mam and Dad,
and takes on all that stress.
When I comes 'ome me little lad just 'ides be'ind 'er dress.
Me daughter looks down at 'er toes an' shakes me by the 'and.
Inside I'm sure she really knows but doesn't understand.

So ask me why I'm going 'ome an' jackin' in this life.
I'm tired o' bein' on me own. I wants to know me wife.
I wants to give the kids the time to know me as their Dad,
So they can't one day say that I'm the one they never 'ad.

I wants to 'elp 'em fly their kite. I wants to dry their eyes,
An' elp 'em get their 'ome-work right, correct 'em when they lies.
I wants to sleep beside me wife an' share the parent's load.
I wants a proper fam'ly life. The kind I never knowed.

So there's the reason's I'm away an' startin' life ashore.
An' soon as I can get me pay you'll not see me no more!
But don't go thinking goin's gonna 'appen easily,
'Cos all the time I'm knowin' that I'm gonna miss the sea.

Been in me veins for far too long to make an easy break.
An' could be that I'm doin' wrong. A chance I 'ave to take.
'Cos when you got a family an' love the sea, you're cursed.
This ocean's got a claim on me. But me wife an' kids comes first.

"Growing up is losing some illusions, in order to acquire others."
...Virginia Woolf

Maturing

When in your eye the glowing fire of freedom has been lit,
And un-tamed winds are dancing in your mane.
When youthful dreams are rattling and champing at the bit,
And young ideals are tugging at the rein.
When restlessly you search for sounds beyond the stable roof
Of distant songs of romance calling low.
And longing for adventure stamps a wild impatient hoof.
Then, my lad, then toss your head and go.

Leap the gate of family ties, yet leave the latch un-harmed,
And gallop where your life would have you roam.
Flare your nostrils wide to scents of wildernesses charmed
With deeds and glories never known at home.
Roll upon the uncut grass of youthful liberty
And canter through the sun-lit vales of love.
Hang your head when whipped by blows of life's reality
And yearn for home when storm clouds pass above.

Bear the load of knowledge being added to your pack.
Accept the halter of maturity.
Never try to throw the weight now saddled to your back,
The burden of responsibility.
And when, though surer footed, than the day you leapt the gate
You slide the latch and walk back to the yard.
Bring your memories home, for, once the stable is your fate,
The harness that you'll wear, my lad, is hard.

"If I have any beliefs about immortality, it is that certain dogs I have known will go to heaven, and very, very few persons."
   ...James Thurber

Old Dickie Dog

And he'll no more cross the bar with me
Beneath the billowed sails.
For he's passed beyond that western sea
Where the water's calm and the trade wind never fails.

Now, while I raise his stiffened leg and place him on the sheet,
I think of the times he used to beg for bones or chunks of meat.
His old paw raised, blind eyes glazed,
His nose would search the scent.
His ancient paw will raise no more.
His time has all been spent.

Now, while I place the links of chain beside his rigid form,
I think of the walks along the docks
when still his breath was warm.
His sailor's stride, legs set wide.
His tilted, stubborn head.
His days have passed before the mast.
Old Dickie Dog is dead.

Now, while I bind the rope around and tug the lashing tight,
I think of the times I woke and found him on my feet at night.
He'd keep the cold from taking hold
When wintry winds would moan.
His warmth is gone, and from here on
We both must sleep alone.

Now, while I row the dinghy out to where the seagulls fly,
I think of the time we ran about, Old Dickie Dog, and I.
He chased the stones, his tired bones
Seemed younger there at play.
But then last night, at dawn's first light,
Old Dickie went away.

Now, as I row back with the tide, a breeze stirs from the west.
And on that breeze the seagulls glide. Old sailor's souls at rest.
One circles slow then swoops so low
Just passing close astern.
Then out to sea. So small. So free.
And never to return.

And he'll no more cross the bar with me
Beneath the billowed sails.
For he's passed beyond that western sea
Where the water's calm and the trade wind never fails.

"Only in the agony of parting do we look into the depths of love."
...George Eliot

It's Best I Leave You While I Can

A poem for you? How hard I tried
But couldn't work one single line.
I wrote instead of a dog that died;
A dog that wasn't even mine.
I loved him though, that ancient hound,
He seemed to understand my ways
Far more than any friend I've found,
Except for you these recent days.

I guess he was a loner too.
That's why he was good company.
I think he'd have accepted you
If time had let him stay with me.
But then, all things must go one day
Upon their own predestined road.
The same as I now go away
From where your tears so freely flowed.

That old dog didn't want to go
But couldn't stop his destiny.
Like me. I think perhaps you know
I'd like to stay. It cannot be.
You see I'm really not the one
That you should want to be with you.
You'll need to find a man who's done
In life those things I'll never do.

For I'm a weary traveling man
Who doubts he'll come to any good.
It's best I leave you while I can
So you can seek the life you should,
Not look at me with eyes that make
Me wish I were no more to roam,
Through tears that cause my heart to break
And strain my soul with dreams of home.

"I've been a long time leaving, but I'm going to be a long time gone."
  ...Willie Nelson

Chapters of Life

So onward once again I tread.
Which way this time? I cannot say,
For one more chapter has been read,
And yet another starts today
Which I must read as best I may
To live the life which lies ahead.

I've still my old companions here
To speed me on the open road:
My rucksack and my silent tear,
My sextant and my heavy load
Of loneliness which always strode
Beside me like a friend most dear.

Though one more memory now have I.
Another follower in my mind
Who'll live there 'till the day I die.
And should I chance to look behind,
I'll maybe see that thought, to find
It makes me stop and softly cry.

For turning back the pages there
I'll find the chapter, thumbing through,
Referring to the places where
You helped me write a page or two.
And then, while glancing back at you
My load may be the less to bear
And onward, once again, I'll tread
To live the life that lies ahead,
'Till every chapter has been read
And every memory is dead.

Shipwreck

Wrecked upon the rock of memory
now my heart must face the storm.
Yearning, like the heart of every man, for havens safe and warm.
Harbours where the heart may rest
from crossing life's uncharted seas,
Replenishing, then sailing west away toward their destinies.

Now no friendly port or crowded harbour waits to welcome me.
Just a lonely weed enshrouded rock amid an empty sea.
There no other soul can sail upon my bow, as would a wife.
Feared are they that tide or gale
may ground them too and wreck their life.

Here I rest, to all a beacon, ringing out to passing hearts
Warnings not to fail or weaken. Not to love if loving starts.
Not at least 'till lines are fast, securely tied to sheltering docks,
Lest the heart may well be cast
aground, as mine, on memories rocks.

Broken there from all the blows
that love and loss contrived to cast.
Praying for a sign which shows that rescue may be sent at last.
Watching while emotions eddy round in swirling, pulling streams.
Cursing these foundations steady. Sailing only in my dreams.

Seeing other hearts approaching, then to veer and sail away.
Only her heart still encroaching, keeping other hearts at bay.
Only her face sailing ever through the oceans of my mind.
Only her love coming never close enough my wreck to find.

"Tis one thing to be tempted, another thing to fall."
...William Shakespeare

In The Face of Temptation

Put away that longing smile you wear.
It bears exciting promise, but it doesn't mean you care.
And though you are a woman I admire
I can't return your loving and I will not be a liar;
My love's already given to the Mother of my kids,
My heart will override temptations loyalty forbids.
Though part of me may wish that I could roam
I won't forsake my family at home.
Too many times they've borne me on
When all my hope was gone
And gave me life.
I'll not forsake my wife!

Though your face is young and free of stress,
Your body bears no marks of children hidden by your dress.
The beauty that you wear is borne by youth,
Though maybe not as pretty hers is borne by seasoned truth.
The lines about her eyes are just reminders of the years
She's given to the kids and me; the laughter, love and tears.
She gave to us her finest time of life.
There's no way I could disrespect my wife.
Through all my trials, and all the pain
She'd build me up again
To rise above.
I won't deceive her love!

Your skin may be more silken and more tan,
And body firm and curved to quench the needs of any man.
Your long luxurious hair flows thick and free
Of greying streaks of aging that adorn my wife and me.
But each grey hair she carries is testament to gain
Achieved by patient motherhood, of loving laced with pain.
And any marks of time her skin may bear
Are living proof of sacrifice and care.
She doesn't hide her age with lies
Her beauty fills my eyes
Like years before.
I don't need anymore!

Yet, if I were a younger man again
I'd have no hesitation. I'd have asked you to remain.
And even now, if I had never wed
I doubtless would have followed where your loving smile had led.
But she sits, quietly waiting, in the home she helped me build,
With laughter and with loving, and our children's lives fulfilled.
She's all a man could ever want in life.
There's no-one with more beauty than my wife.
Whatever marks of time she bears
Or scars of age she wears
I cannot see.
She's beautiful to me!

"Faith transcends reason. It is when the horizon is the darkest and human reason is beaten down to the ground that faith shines brightest and comes to our rescue."
...Mohandas (Mahatma) Gandhi

The Call

It always seemed I'd never any time to be their Dad,
My job had interrupted almost every plan we'd had.
But this time I had promised them to go out for the day;
We'd load the boat and quietly sail away.
We put aboard the fishing gear and iced the drinks down cold,
My two boys hanked the heads'ls on like sailor folk of old.
My daughter set the galley straight so nothing there could fall.
I smiled and thought looks like they've learned it all.

The pride I felt inside me, as those three secured for sea,
It almost broke my heart to think they'd learned it all for me.
I knew that day they'd come to love the ocean and its ways
And understand their Father's absent days.
I started up the engine while they did what they should do,
I didn't need to say a word, those kids already knew.
No time at all, the fenders stowed, the lines all coiled and hung.
Such confidence is rare in ones so young.

We'd cleared the bar and turned her
when the pager made it's noise.
My daughter stopped and stared toward the older of the boys.
He looked at me without a word. The laughter now was gone.
His eyes were asking me to motor on.
The message called out urgently, they needed me at base.
My little girl had turned to hide the tears now on her face.
Her older brother held her as he tried hard to explain.
I turned the bow toward the dock again.

Now silently they made her fast and stowed the gear below.
My youngest lad was crying now because I had to go.
I picked him up and carried him to where the others stood
And tried to comfort them as best I could.
I called the base to find out why they needed me so bad.
They said a boat was sinking with three children and their Dad.
And when I worked their chances out my soul began to groan.
Those kids were just the same age as my own.

I asked for their position and was told they weren't too sure,
But figured they were close to where that ferry sank before.
My mind went cold as I recalled that rescue in the dark,
The night I lost the skipper to a shark.
I told the base to mobilize all boats and all the crew.
I'd run in my own boat and get there sooner than they'd do.
They asked who I'd be running with, what crew I had to go.
I said I'd have the finest crew I know.

I ran to where the children stood and told them of the call.
They didn't question anything. They understood it all.
We left the dock and motored out as fast as she could go
To find those kids before they sank below.
I pushed the engine harder than she'd ever gone, then more.
And all I thought was those could be my kids we're searching for.
My eldest took the look-out sitting half way up the mast.
My daughter told the boat it must go fast.

We'd raced through Ragged Channel
and were running past The Lee,
My eldest spotted something
though not sure what he could see.
The shape he saw there tossing didn't look much like a boat.
But at least, if it was them, it was afloat!
My lass unlashed the life-ring and she flaked the line on deck.
My youngest came from down below,
two life vests round his neck.
My eldest climbed back down and tied the fenders on a line.
I felt so proud those island kids were mine!

We closed the hulk and realized was just her bow was clear.
I couldn't see survivors as we carefully drew near.
My daughter shouted "Daddy, I see someone by the rail!"
I saw the little boy alone and pale.
My heart was now exploding! We had found the youngest son.
But what about the others? Could he be the only one?
Were they inside? Or drifted off? Or taken by a shark?
Just like that ferry skipper in the dark.

As we closed and moved up-wind to toss the lad a float
We saw two others holding tight to windward of the boat.
I called to them instructions and the Father's voice replied
Telling us his girl was still inside.
I looked at my own daughter 'till my sight was blurred with tears
And thought if that was her in there, and other nameless fears.
She took my hand and squeezed it tight,
she somehow seemed to know.
She told me that I had to go below.

We pulled the boys aboard, their Dad had said he wouldn't leave.
I couldn't tell if he still hoped or wanted just to grieve.
His eldest said she's tapping on the hull, but getting weak.
I tried to ask him more, but couldn't speak.
I told my eldest lad to take the wheel and stand to lee.
I knew he'd get them home if something happened there to me.
I grabbed my mask, strapped on my knife
and swam toward the wreck,
My children watching silent from the deck.

The father was exhausted but he had to lend a hand!
I barked at him some orders which I hoped he'd understand.
The first time that I went below and saw the way things stood
I knew my chance of winning wasn't good.
The deck hatch was the only passage in and out of there.
As soon as it was opened we'd be spilling all the air.
It wouldn't take so long before she'd slide beneath the waves
To take those still inside her to their graves.

The sea was way too rough for us to lash her to our side.
I couldn't see another plan, though God! I know I tried!
With every wave that rocked her, bubbles eased from every vent.
I'd hardly any time before she went!
I lashed a line about the mast and measured off a length,
Filled my lungs to breaking point. Prayed I'd have the strength!
And went below full knowing there I'd more than likely stay.
I prayed my kids would understand that day!

The hatch swung open easily, I lashed it to the mast
And swam inside and prayed again my breath was going to last.
But the fo'c's'le cabin door was jammed
with no time left to spare.
Should I stay or go back up for air?
I knew there'd be no second chance. She'd start to sink before.
I knew there should be air still trapped beyond that cabin door.
Was then I heard my daughter urge me on to save a life.
My doubt was gone, I reached down for my knife!

At first there was no movement, then the door began to give.
My lungs were just about to burst, I'd little time to live!
At last it gave completely. I lunged toward the bow
And prayed that there would still be air there now
My head broke through the surface and I gasped a fearful breath.
I don't think I had ever come as close to certain death.
A frightened whimper next to me was music to my ears.
She's still alive! I cursed my selfish fears.

I couldn't see her face at all, that tiny space was black.
I found her hand and told her we would soon be swimming back.
She sobbed and said she couldn't swim
and asked if she would die.
I told her not while I was so close by!
I felt the boat begin to slide! The surface seemed to rise!
I knew we'd only seconds left. I'd no more time for lies.
I told her take your deepest breath, then do it once again.
And prayed my will could both of us sustain.

I clamped my hand across her mouth and covered up her nose,
And pulled her to my body while the water level rose.
And pulled us both back under then toward the cabin door
And begged my lungs to battle on once more.
We cleared the door, I kicked toward the hatch's pale light.
The girl though struggling feebly was far too weak to fight.
And as we cleared the coaming
and I thought were free from harm,
She hung there limp and lifeless on my arm.

I didn't think a boat would sink as fast as she'd gone down.
The surface was too far away. I knew we both would drown.
Then thought my kids are up there and I owe them one last try,
And started kicking up toward the sky.
The last that I remember was the surface turning black,
And feeling something powerful was tugging at my back.
I thought that must be Satan, and my soul is up for bids
For times a should have been there for my kids,

And then I saw a stranger's face, and heard him call my name.
Then several other voices all were calling me, the same.
Then my eldest lad was asking if I was OK,
My daughter said they thought I'd gone away.
Before my mind could work things out
a friend's face came in view.
We'd sailed together often on the search and rescue crew.
I asked him of the little girl, he said she'd be alright.
She'd have to stay in hospital tonight.

They helped me sit and propped me up.
My children gathered round.
I asked them what had happened, how come I hadn't drowned.
The crew agreed I should have for the idiot I'd been,
But not the one whose face I hadn't seen.
He shook my hand quite slowly, looked me steady in the eye.
I couldn't gauge his feeling, though he seemed as if to cry.
And then I recognized him as the father of the child.
I thanked him then. Silently he smiled.

He asked my why I thanked him,
though I guessed he really knew.
His face had told me everything his words would never do.
I thanked him for his gratitude, and thanked him for his pain,
For loving that young lass he'd see again.
And then the others told me of events I didn't know.
Just after I had gone below there'd really been a show.
The rescue boat had come on scene just as I went inside.
And that's why neither one of us had died.

While speaking on the radio I'd told them all I should.
And, knowing the situation, they'd prepared as best they could.
They'd seen the boat slide under and had divers standing by,
Who saw me start to kick toward the sky.
They'd reached me as my lungs gave out
and darkness filled my brain.
And took from me the drowning child and bore us up again.
They'd plugged me to a mouthpiece
and then forced a feeble breath,
And brought me back to life from certain death.

A coast-guard chopper took the lass as soon as she was clear.
Their medics gave her CPR, but still it had been near!
They'd dragged me on the rescue boat
and worked on me some more
Until I barfed my guts out on the floor.
My boys had helped the other's sons
and clothed them with their own.
My little lass was steering like a person fully grown.
They'd lifted me to my own deck and laid me at the stern.
Then called my wife to tell of our return.

I took my daughters hand in mine, and told her what I'd heard.
That when I went inside the bow, I'd done it on her word.
I could have turned and surfaced, but she'd asked me to remain
And bring the little child back again.
She didn't seem surprised, in fact she quietly said she knew.
She said she'd been there with me
during all that I'd been through.
And said she heard me pray to God each time I was in doubt.
And felt my pain when lungs, and hope, gave out.

I held her close and cried into her golden flowing hair.
She'd understood it all. Could she really have been there?
From deep inside I vowed that I would organize my life
To spend more time ashore with kids and wife.
She told me not to worry, they now understood my ways.
The nights out on the ocean, the many absent days.
And then she said that if I changed, I wouldn't still be me,
The only way they want their Dad to be.
She told me I must stay upon the sea.
And prayed that it would also one day be her destiny.

"What do we live for, if not to make life less difficult for each other."
...George Eliot

Choices

Those quiet inner voices had started then to show
How you should make the choices
of where your heart should go.
You'd never guessed the gentle man
You hoped would help you heal and plan
Would so confuse the clarity you sought.
He'd helped your understanding, and shared your ancient pain,
Then, through your heart's demanding, you'd looked at him again
And found a depth you'd never known,
A man at peace, though so alone,
Yet one who seemed to comprehend your thought.

He steered your frail emotions toward more solid ground;
Encouraged your devotions to those whose lives were bound
So close with yours through childhood need.
He never slowed, but rather freed
Your soul to share itself with those you'd choose.
Yet slowly you were learning that his soul was the one
With whom your own was yearning to quietly start to run.
And though you fought that thought, you lost
And, knowing not what be the cost,
You chose this man to share with, win or lose.

He hadn't the intention to be more than a friend,
Yet added a dimension you hoped would never end.
His simple world from nature's laws
So complemented those of yours
That corporate and city life had spawned.
You found in him a grounding when all else seemed confused.
And felt yourself rebounding from where you'd been abused
To where you saw those dreams you'd dreamed
Were never lost as they had seemed,
But waiting 'till this day of sharing dawned.

And so, without forgetting, you put your past behind,
As onward now you're setting to seek what you might find.
And up ahead he quietly stands
With gentle heart and open hands
And looking on to where your path may lead.
Now as you stand beside him, the winds dance through your hair,
You wonder should you guide him, or let him take you there.
Then, slow at first, you match his stride
To walk together side by side,
To find what life now holds, forever freed.

Requiem

Another day departed, and with it *she* is gone.
Her journey, long since started, once more has traveled on
To distant lands beyond our sight. To just the other side of night
Where dawn is always waiting, bright and pure.
She wouldn't want our sorrow, nor have us know the pain
That come the next tomorrow she'd be not here again,
So thus, though gone, her warmth will stay
to walk with us another day.
To help the one's she loved so well endure.

We feel her close around us. We sense her silent breath.
We know the love that bound us cannot be lost to death.
We know that ere we walk this earth,
the one who chose to give us birth
Remains in every step our lives will take.
Beyond the unseen ranges though now her feet may tread,
Her love shall bear no changes, our hearts need bear no dread.
For she's prepared us well to live.
To love. To laugh. To freely give.
To learn, not run, from each mistake we'll make.

Now sailed beyond our vision, to reach another shore.
Accomplished in the mission she chose to come here for.
Completing well her earthly tasks,
she's gone to where her spirit asks
That she may help some others find their way.
We watched while she was leaving 'till gone from mortal view.
Though sad, we were not grieving, for something in us knew
That though her earthly life be done,
as ours her path has just begun
…And paths will cross again…
…Another day…

"You have to do your own growing, no matter how tall your grandfather was."
...Abraham Lincoln

A Man 'Mongst Other Men

I signed on that old sailing ship to find meself a life.
Too wise by far for schoolin', and too young to want no wife.
But if I'd known what I'd go through once we 'ad left the shore
I never would 'ave walked out o' that door.

No more was I than sixteen year, though sure I was full grown.
I'd only worked the farms before I set out on me own.
A cocky kid who never did but 'ang around at 'ome.
Who never should 'ave chose to try to roam.

I packed up me belongin's though, which didn't take too long.
And packed me past be'ind me too, which didn't seem so wrong,
And 'itched a ride to catch the tide and 'elped cast off the line,
And wondered 'bout this brand new life o' mine.

Well that was nineteen month ago, and just now I returned.
I've scars across me broken nose, and manhood truly earned.
Me knuckles, too, is scarred and blue. I gave as good as took.
And learned more from that ship than any book.

I'd nineteen months o' purgat'ry, which made that kid a man.
And learned to fight for what was mine, and not once have I ran.
And give 'em due, I lost a few before I learned to win.
But never let them think I might give in.

I started at the bottom and right there I would 'ave stayed
'Ad I not figured pretty quick to show I'm not afraid.
And though I might 'ave lost the fight, that first and painful time,
'Twas then my social rank began to climb.

I 'ad to prove meself the worth o' those what give me 'ell.
And win respect for shovin' back, not runnin' off to tell.
And once I learned that what I'd earned bore rough-cut dignity,
I also earned the rough respect o' me.

So 'ere I stands at eighteen year, a man who'll look you straight,
With shoulders o' the farm boy, and the knuckles o' the mate.
I've earned me pride on soil and tide and like what I became.
For that old ship don't let you stay the same.

And now I'm signin' off and then I'm 'eading for the land.
I'll cuss me shipmates one more time and shake 'em by the 'and.
Then 'oist me pack high on me back and walk up to the farm,
And show me worried mum I met no 'arm.

I'll go back to the lambing sheds, the milk barn and the plough.
I've been to find adventure and I've 'ad me fill for now.
I'll study then at school again, and build meself a life,
And start to find the lass to be me wife.

I still owe that old schooner, though God knows I paid me dues.
She taught me what no school can teach, in ways that I can use.
She taught me when 'mongst other men to show that I'm a man,
And why, and how, and 'specially that I can.

That creakin' leakin' schooner at the call o' wind and tide,
She scoured that stupid wide-eyed kid and found the man inside.
And took 'im 'alf way round the world,
and dropped 'im at the door
He'll never need to leave from any more.
She took 'im 'alf way round the world,
and brought 'im 'ome agen…
The boy no more; for evermore a man 'mongst other men!

"Men succeed when they realize that their failures are the preparation for their victories."
    ...Ralph Waldo Emerson

Preparation

Me it was I thought that formed my past
Leaving through the door of sought adventure.
Setting out at youth before the mast,
Cast upon the sea by bound indenture.
So was set the pattern for my years,
Never knowing quite what lay ahead.
Tossed between my passions and my tears.
Lost between my vision and my dread.

So it was I traveled every land,
Building on experience and wonder.
Never with the wit to understand
Why my dreams were wrecked and rent asunder.
Why a home was never so for long.
Why good friends seemed always far behind.
How by doing right I was so wrong.
Why the truth was never mine to find.

Questions thus I bore within my soul
Searching every path for explanation.
Never knowing quite my destined role.
Recognizing only trepidation.
Still I never turned to follow back
Down toward from where this path began.
Still I faced in turn each unknown track
Never knowing where, or why, they ran.

Only when I came upon this war
Reason showed its light through my confusion.
Slow I learned what I was put here for.
Slow reality replaced illusion.
All those scattered strings began to weave
Intricate designs of common sense.
All those times I fought and wouldn't leave
Joined to form the core of my defense.

All that pain I'd felt and loss I'd seen
Joined to forge the shield of my protection.
All these desperate places I have been
Served to give me reference for reflection.
All the times I've witnessed virtue fall
Strengthened my resolve to help it rise.
All the doubts I've wrestled through it all
Now have cleared my conscience, and my eyes.

Set am I to face what lies ahead
Strong of spirit, strong of heart and sinew.
Casting down the treason of my dread.
Realizing that which life puts in you
Waits for just such moments to appear.
Times when threat and challenge must be met.
Now such time draws imminently near,
Mine shall be the fight without regret.

Mine shall be the parry to the thrust.
Standing to the line which holds undaunted.
Mine shall be the truth that all can trust
Though all rules and justices be flaunted.
Mine shall be the hand that bears the light
Onward through the darkest of the fray,
Leading forth through never ending night,
On toward the dawning of the day.

Thus my past has rallied to the cause
Standing at my side with silent power
Won from fighting through a life of wars.
Training, so it seems, for just this hour.
Thus I draw this sword and heft this shield
Knowing now I no more stand alone.
Rank on rank beside me in the field
Marches each experience I've known.

This was why I suffered every blow.
This was why life barred each tried ambition.
Though I never chose the ways to go,
Now I see the purpose of this mission.
Now I understand why times were tough.
Why each challenge threatened to destroy.
Now, when other men would cry "enough!"
Here I have an army to deploy.

Then, had my life been as I'd desired,
Surely now I'd run, my will depleted.
Here instead, in battle garb attired,
Rides this noble phalanx undefeated.
Then, had I not carried every weight,
Born each disappointment, loss and pain,
Surely now I'd run, not face this fate,
Fighting on, and fighting on again.

Praise be sung to forces I'll not know,
Even though they gave no explanation,
Making hard the ways I'd choose to go.
Making of my life this preparation.
Teaching me the laws I couldn't learn
Should I live a hundred normal lives.
Helping me, unwittingly, to earn
Values he possesses who survives.

Though I ride this day to meet my foe,
Armed with all I need for certain glory,
Still one learning yet I need to know
Ere we close the book upon this story.
That, when victory be in my reach,
Enemies be set to meet their end,
Was the lesson learned which tried to teach,
"Conquer, and then make of foe a friend."

Could that I have learned too much from loss,
Blinding me from basic humble virtue?
Can I yet that battle line un-cross
Saying, "Though I've won, I will not hurt you."
May all learning from my past allow
Sword to be replaced with open hand?
Can I win a peace where, even now,
Foe, though vanquished well, may freely stand?
Have these lessons yet that made me strong
Also taught me well this victor's cost?
Or, though being right, shall I prove wrong?
Winning just a hardened soul that's lost.

"When the earth is sick, the animals will begin to disappear, when that happens the warriors of the rainbow will come to save them."
...Chief Seattle

An End to Freedom

There upon the hill I see it spattered;
Thin red trail of life about to fade.
Paw prints in the powdered snow, the only other mark to show
Where this once noble creature quietly laid.
Though my life and dreams have now been shattered,
Still I must conclude this cruel deed.
Following that bloody spoor, I pray I'll find him well before
His spirit goes to where it can't be freed.

We'd survived alone with few possessions.
Me my bow, and him his stealth and speed.
Both had years of hard earned skill,
but neither one would ever kill
The more than we could carry, eat or need.
Sometimes I would see his paw's impressions.
Often he would catch my wind-borne scent.
Once or twice I caught his eye.
We'd watch as brothers, passing by,
But never go the way the other went.

Then the settlers came upon these ranges.
Bringing foreign beasts and different ways.
We'd been living high and free.
The land was shared by him and me
While spirits watched us from the ancient days.
Soon we saw the first of many changes.
Trees were felled and streams were damned and filled.
Game was mercilessly shot, and left, most often, there to rot
Upon the blood stained land where it was killed.

Soon there was so little food for killing.
That first winter left us nearly dead.
He and I both quietly knew the land would no more carry two
Both needing to be regularly fed.
First we shared, as brothers, true and willing.
Each would leave some kill to feed his friend.
Then the railway pushing west
dispersed the herds, and killed the rest,
We knew our time was coming to an end.

Late at night a Manitou would find me.
Speak the ancient words I knew were true.
Steady came the quiet voice to tell me I must make the choice
To live as then and die, or start anew.
Waking dreams kept trying to remind me
I must help my brother stay alive.
With him now my spirit ran, but there within the time of man
I knew he was too gentle to survive.

So I left my hills and spirit brother,
Hoping without me he'd find more food.
That was all I had to give. My freedom, so that he might live.
My noble past to join this savage brood.
There I tried to live as someone other.
Learn their selfish ways my soul decried.
'Till my spirit screamed aloud
to tell my heart, once strong, once proud,
How fast my soul had strangled there, and died.

That was when I walked back to the ranges.
Bow upon my back and knife to hand.
That was when I heard the gun and saw my brother fall, then run.
And that was when I came to understand.
There are some who'll never live with changes.
There are some who's freedom they can't give.
Him and me, our souls must fly forever 'tween the grass and sky
Where savagery of man could never live.

Passing then the two who shot my brother,
Hearing then their mocking of my friend,
Boasting he would die in pain, no more to kill a calf again.
I gave to them a fast and peaceful end.
May they find forgiveness from Our Mother,
May their haunted spirits lie at rest.
One with eye's yet open wide,
his throat now slit from side to side,
The other with my arrow in his chest.

Now upon the hill I see them spattered.
All my brother's hopes before they died.
Paw prints in the powdered snow, the only other mark to show
Where this once noble creature quietly cried.
Now with my hope destitute and shattered,
I must let my brother's spirit free.
Following that bloody spoor, I have to free his soul before
I turn the knife and do the same to me.

"The biggest disease today is not leprosy or tuberculosis, but rather the feeling of being unwanted."
...Mother Teresa

The Last Tripper

He's drinking himself to death, poor sod!
That's how it effects some blokes.
He can't see a future and can't see his God,
And outlived the last of his folks!
He's old and used. Tired. Confused.
He's finished, but can't reason why.
The company don't want him. He don't want himself!
He's hazard to shipping! He's hazard to health!
So why don't he bloody well die?
He's still got some natural will to survive
And that's all that keeps him alive.

He's worked with the sea all his life, poor sod!
He started when they had sails!
He rounded Australia, fished off Cape Cod,
And told us some marvelous tales
Of oceans and shores, sailors and wars,
And ships…but that's all in his past.
He's telling them now to the glass in his hand
And shaking his head like he can't understand…
Nigh fifty years under the mast!
And what'll he get for that life that is lost?
His pension can't cover that cost!

He's crying now in his drink, poor sod!
The way that a baby would.
He's catching his past in a wet paper wad,
But tears can't do any good,
'Cos time moves on, and his has gone,
And he hasn't a clue where it went.
He can't turn his life back to where it began,
But wants to. And want to believe that he can
'Cos he's figured his time's about spent.
If he's lucky retirement won't hang around
Before he gets heaven bound.

He's drinking himself to death, poor sod!
And seems like he's doing it right.
Although it looks bad, it doesn't seem odd.
He's just a pathetic sight!
His whiskey breath now stinks of death.
He's killing some more every day!
What ever the money he's managed to save
Should cover the cost of his near empty grave
And the people that cart him away.
And I wonder if ever a tear will be shed
When finally he's drunk himself dead?

"Some die too young, some die too old; the precept sounds strange, but die at the right age."
... Friedrich Nietzsche

Back From The Light

Come near, my children, bring your light
To glow amid this morbid gloom.
Dispel the portents of this night
Whose shadows shroud this solemn room.
The gentle flame of love you bring
Shall cause to stay this death foretold
By learned men with words that sing
Of time so come to one not old.

Come near instead to hear my song
For you have yet no right to grieve.
Their words sound wise, but they are wrong;
My time is not yet come to leave.
My song, the universe does write,
And sings it loud on nature's breath.
It bears no fears of fading light,
But hopes of one returned from death.

Come near, so you my voice can hear,
And mind not that it whispers so.
And dry that bravely hidden tear
For I am not about to go.
Though blood be thin and muscle weak
Your love my spirit has reborn.
'Tis not your tears this night shall seek,
But laughter on the morrow's dawn.

Come near and take this withered hand
That once, and yet, would grasp so strong.
And know again, at my command,
There pen and sword will soon belong.
And know that, though I've seen the end
And borne its fell and fearful pain,
What was that foe is now the friend
Who forged this will to live again.

Come near and take one final look
On death, before it's turned aside
From one life less its clutches took;
From one life more that hasn't died.
For come the time the sun shall wake
No bell my sad demise will toll.
I've still too much of life to make
To let death sever heart from soul.

Now go and sleep this night content
That yet we'll share life's open road.
That yet my sojourn isn't spent
Upon this earthly path I strode.
Know too that I did see so clear
The beauty that's awaiting me.
Yet turned and, smiling, came back here
To seek my unfound destiny
Among the ones I hold most dear.
For now I bear no mortal fear
Of death, and tell eternity
To wait, just one more life, for me
To claim my immortality.

"The truth is, of course, that there is no journey. We are arriving and departing all at the same time."
...David Bowie

The White Dove

Beyond the last haven a white dove is flying
From shore, to a white ship with billowing sails
That rides on the breeze from where evening is dying
O'er the sea to the West where the light never fails.

We stand on the beach and watch her departing
And share in the sadness her leaving has brought,
We smile as we know that her voyage, now starting,
Will bear her to lands beyond our mortal thought

Where she'll meet the loved ones
who've sailed o'er these waters
And wait now to welcome her home once again,
On white shores where parents rejoin with their daughters
In a place with no sorrow, in a land with no pain.

There she will stay amid sunlight and laughter,
And love and contentment with never a care,
To wait for each one of us following after
To sail o'er those waters and join with her there.

And as we lose sight of that lonely ship gliding
Below the horizon so far from our shore,
She rises above, on the fresh breeze she's riding
To come into view of all those gone before.

While we wave farewell through tears at her leaving,
And quietly remember the one that we love,
A white ship nears land that knows not of grieving
And to shore flies a beautiful, peaceful white dove.

"Learn from the mistakes of others. You can't live long enough to make them all yourself."
...Eleanor Roosevelt

Learn Well from the Lessons I can Give

Please, sit beside me traveler of the road.
I'd like to share some lessons that I've learned.
There's some that life, unasked for, freely showed.
And others, more important, that were mercilessly earned.

And some have cost me dear in pain of heart,
Which still I never heed at passion's call.
Despite the recognition, I yet start
Upon that costly climb from which I always seem to fall.

And some have lost me friendships held so dear
When selfishness outbid the will to share.
Now, though doubtless far more wise, I fear
That mine is yet a poorer life without such friends to care.

And some have left me overcome with guilt,
So born from my dishonour and my shame
Which undermined the pinnacles I'd built
And turned me from the man I was to what I then became.

And some have drained my soul of any pride
So earned as each endeavour would succeed,
When looking at the one's I cast aside
To further my career and satisfy my heartless greed.

And some have forced me now to look behind
To see the path which led to where we met.
To show me how my conscience had been blind.
Though now to see so clearly all I struggle to forget.

Fair traveler, you've never heard my name,
Nor likely will you know me when we part.
Our roads that brought us here were not the same
Nor will they be so when our onward journeys shall restart.

So learn well from the lessons I can give,
For many have your wayward life not taught.
Avoid the pointless pains I've had to live,
And seek you not the futile grails my wasted days have sought.

Please, learn well from the lessons I can give,
But also teach me yours from deed and thought,
That I may learn how days I've yet to live
Can turn to something other than a life which comes to naught.

"The mind that is wise mourns less for what age takes away; than what it leaves behind."
...William Wordsworth

Rights of Passage

Only when you've journeyed to your spirit's farthest reaches,
Met each mortal challenge and then challenged them again.
Only when you've learned the laws of life that journey teaches,
Then, and only then, may you be heard midst other men

Only when you've spent each ounce of will still left inside you,
Then to find you yet had more from somewhere deep within.
Only when you've recognized the strengths
you'd thought denied you,
Then, and only then, your road to manhood may begin.

Only when you've overcome the doubts each step is showing,
Turned them into certainties, or cast them from your mind.
Only when you learn to trust the wisdom that is growing,
Then, and only then, may you leave boyhood years behind.

Only when your heart is scarred from pains life casts around you.
Back is bent from burdens and your head with sorrow hung.
Only when experience leaves little to astound you,
Then, and only then, may you appreciate the young.

The Aftermath

Children, quietly pray, who then had cried.
The world seems silent now the storm has passed.
Friends all ask each other who has died.
And thank their God it's gone...it's gone at last!

Jagged rafters frame the morning stars
Where once a roof had hid the threatening night.
Broken hulls lie tangled with their spars
Among the reefs six fathom out of sight.

Poles and trees lay felled across a lane.
Sea debris in puddles by the school.
Once a garden moistened by the rain,
Now a tragic waste-land, torn and cruel.

Church still stands though now its bell is gone
That rang out nature's fury at its height
To fall among the ancient graves upon
The only souls who rested through that night.

Kitten, sodden, drowned beneath a porch.
Car lies smashed and twisted in the rain.
A mother calls a name and shines a torch,
Hopes to find her children's dog again.

Rooster floating, bobbing on the waves.
Sunken head no more to cry the day.
Now he silent crows the watery graves
Of those the parting storm has washed away.

Slowly, through the dark and frightened dawn
Cautiously, the ones who yet can tread,
Pick their way through wreckage, tired and worn,
Searching for the living...Or the dead.

Grief... Relief... The long night now is done.
Glory was not earned by those who fought.
Victory was not for those who won.
Loss the only prize this battle bought.

"Can miles truly separate you from friends? If you want to be with someone you love, aren't you already there?"
...Richard Bach

Souls in Love Apart

Physical laws cannot contain emotion,
Time and distance cannot cage the heart,
Neither mountain range nor deepest ocean
Yet shall keep two souls that love apart.
For love is of the spirit, not of matter
Born within the soul it has no frame.
However far two hearts in love may scatter
Still they stay united just the same.

However many miles they put between them
Still they'll share the bonds that used to be,
However long it's been since each has seen them
Matters not if love's their destiny.
Where uncorrupted love has once existed,
Despite the trials of time, it shall sustain.
And separation's doubts shall be resisted
Until they both can be as one again.

For physical laws cannot contain emotion,
Time and distance cannot cage the heart.
There is no mountain range or rolling ocean
   Yet can keep two souls, in love, apart.

"In seed time learn, in harvest teach, in winter enjoy."
...William Blake

For the Seasons Come and Go

Now the trees upon the ridge shed their autumn shrouds.
See the fallen red and gold. Feel the nights start turning cold.
Bring the blankets from the drawer.
Watch those northern clouds,
Now the nights are getting longer every day.
Fetch the cordwood from the yard to a dryer space.
Check the water pipes won't freeze.
Feel the sharp edge on the breeze.
Take your son on one last camp to your favourite place,
Then put canoes and summer thoughts away.

For the seasons come and go,
And you have to take the changes as they turn.
Winter freeze or summer burn.
When the warmth has turned to snow
You should have the winter planned out in your mind.
You should never fall behind
For the seasons won't be kind if you don't learn.

Bring the snow plough from the barn to the garage door.
Buy the wife another fleece.
Watch the southbound flights of geese.
Lay the feed in for the herd, order plenty more
For the weather channel's warnings are severe.
Feel the ground start turning hard when the rains don't fall.
See the silver on the lawn glisten more with every dawn.
Watch the squirrels build their nests. Hear the ravens call,
Telling soon will be the ending of the year.

For the seasons come and go
And you have to change to suit their different needs.
Reap your crops or plant your seeds.
And their moods you have to know
For you must obey each law that they command
And you have to understand
That when nature makes demands you can't be slow.

So zip the lining in your coat. Bring the seedlings in.
Check the lad's boots aren't your own,
for his feet have surely grown.
See the salt trucks standing by as the snows begin.
Think of everything you still might need to do.
For your parents taught you well, through your growing days,
As you learned of nature's truth,
through the lessons of your youth.
So bring your boy up to the fire, teach him well those ways,
The time is come for him to know them too.

For the seasons come and go
And the same as summer sun gives way to frost
So young innocence is lost,
And each year your son will grow
'Till the day when he'll be standing on his own,
Facing winter's cold alone,
Giving thanks that he was shown all he should know.

So now prepare him for that time as the seasons turn.
Fill his head with what you can. That'll help him be a man
Show him well at every chance all he'll need to learn,
For the winter will be here before you know.
Watch him grow to be so tall; breath a saddened sigh.
Once you've helped him all you can
you must follow nature's plan,
And shake his hand and turn away as he says good bye.
For like summer's warmth in fall he's bound to go.

For the seasons come and go
And you feel that just as autumn's turning cold,
So your life is growing old.
Then the time has come to know
That you better have your winter stock in store.
For your summer is no more
As the chill winds at your door begin to blow.
And you wonder when your time will come to go.

"Do not go where the path may lead; go instead where there is no path and leave a trail"
...Ralph Waldo Emerson

The Last Portage

We came down that winding path together,
Just like all those trails we've walked before.
Traveling so far away, I never thought we'd face the day
When there were no more trails we might explore.
Wandering through all terrains and weather,
You and I just faced the track ahead.
Turn on turn we shared the load
to help each other down that road
Though neither one was knowing where it led.

Now we face this shore that lies before us.
Load our aged packs aboard again.
Easy now they seem to stow,
as if themselves they seem to know
The place where they so many times have lain.
Here beside the waters that first bore us
We now turn to see the path behind.
Only to that final bend, so close upon our journey's end,
Is all our tired eyes will ever find.

That's the last portage we're making.
The last load we'll bear.
That's the last path we're taking.
The last trail we'll share.

Back beyond that bend our pasts lay waiting,
Lives too rich and full to understand.
All those years have come and gone
since you and I first set upon
Our journey through this vast and untamed land.
Knowing why we both are hesitating,
Eyes now locked together wise and stern.
Back beyond that bend we're free,
but what awaits us, you and me,
Upon the other shore once we return?

Looking where the city's lights are burning,
Casting their reflections on the lake.
Standing silent, side by side. Neither one can try to hide
The tears born from the choice we now must make.
Stepping from the shadows of our yearning,
One last firm embrace before we go.
Never now to look behind we launch to face what we must find
Upon that distant shore we once did know.

That's the last portage we're making.
The last load we'll bear.
That's the last path we're taking.
The last trail we'll share.

"If you want a happy ending that depends, of course, on where you stop your story"
...Orson Welles

The Ending

In passions of beginning, accelerating thought,
Our dreams of love were spinning
the webs in which were caught
The hopes that should have born us on
toward the life that now is gone.
The life that never was, nor could have been.
It died before conception. Before it witnessed light.
Devoid of loves affection in solitary night
The quiet words we tried to speak
of what it was we'd strive to seek
Were never heard, and tears were never seen.

Our lives were lived in lying. Hiding what was true.
Consciences denying, everything we knew
Of all the years that lay behind,
with scarce a smile that we could find.
With scarce a word that we might try again.
And knowing it was ending we turned upon the past
Exhausted from pretending that we might make it last.
We turned upon the dreams we dreamed
with hatred for their lies which seemed
To magnify our anger and our pain.

So now as we're departing from what our dreams became.
Alone, are we restarting, or merely just the same?
Though traveling now by different ways
through different lives, the future stays
A product of the differences we shared.
We'll walk in two directions, impossible to cross.
We'll bear our own reflections of compromise and loss.
And given up we can't look back
to where we left the severed track,
Nor where we joined…to see how much we cared…
…When passions of beginning, accelerated thought,
When dreams of love were spinning the
webs in which were caught
The hopes that should have born us on…
… toward the life that now is gone.

"We are prone to judge success by the index of our salaries or the size of our automobiles, rather than by the quality of our service relationship to humanity."
...Dr. Martin Luther King, Jr.

The Volunteers

Dedicated to the men and women of
Virgin Islands Search and Rescue (V.I.S.A.R.)

When you've scrutinized the concept,
and examined those who try
And you've understood their efforts and their aim,
And you've spoken to the ones
who called for help, and didn't die,
You'll be pleased with what those selfless folk became.
Though they're only volunteers with resources all too few
They have answered every call that they've received.
When few of us respond to those in trouble as they do,
Their commitment's sometimes hard to be believed.

At first they were accused of being some private members club,
Though membership is open to all who want to save lives at sea!
But they're only doing this country's work
when they'd rather be down the pub!
So give them a hand for this country's sake …
… They work for free!

They've spouses and often children
who will worry through the night,
And partners, friends, employers through the day,
All asking if the ones they need will make it back all-right,
And why they risk their lives for zero pay?
'Cos they're only volunteers doing all to save a life,
Not for glory, but because they just can do it!
And they have to make that sacrifice to husband, boss or wife,
Who they hope will understand and help them through it.

They're fathers, they are lovers,
they are workers, mums and wives,
And all have got commitments and should really be elsewhere!
But they're only doing this country's work,
and would rather live quieter lives!
So help them help for this country's sake …
…And let them care!

There's those who try to breath back life,
and some who drive the boat,
A few who'll talk with relatives to calm them.
And those who raise the funds to keep the rescue teams afloat.
Yet more who teach to kids how things can harm them.
But they're only volunteers, and they'll not ask any thanks
'Cos they're happy just to know they contributed.
And there's not a single hero can be counted in their ranks.
So let's not let their motives be disputed!

They're a builder, they're a banker, or a fisherman or flyer,
Surprisingly they're just like you; they care some… so they give!
They want to be doing this county's work,
but rather that work were dryer,
So help them give for this country's sake…
…It's here they live!

We all live next to nature, and her prodigy, the sea,
Which touches all our lives, our days, our hours!
It's us, no matter who we are. It's you, or they, or me,
Who has to deal with her destructive powers!
And them? They're only volunteers
and most of them are strangers
If thinking of the place from where they've moved.
But they're the ones who face the threat
despite the present dangers!
Anonymous and often unapproved.

Whether foreigner or local, whether millionaire or fool,
It doesn't matter who you are, what nation, wealth or creed!
If you need them to do this country's work
they only obey one rule,
So cheer them on for this country's sake...
...And bid "God's speed!"

(With respect for Rudyard Kipling's "The Absent Minded Beggar"
from which the form was borrowed)

"Our sorrows and wounds are healed only when we touch them with compassion."
...Buddha

Friendly Fire

Quietly I've watched your injured heart,
And longed to feel the trusting in your damaged soul restart.
Gently I have searched within your eyes
And seen the marks of loss you bear from all the pain and lies.
For you've been scarred by fires of love without return.
And suffer from the agonies their smoldering embers burn.
So now within the warmth your soul should claim
Flare memories of love's destructive flame.

The lesson that your heart has learned
From having all you trusted burned inside,
Was love must be denied.

Somehow I must take your timid hand
And show you that a man can gently care and understand.
Slowly I must build within your mind
The thought that what's before you needn't be what lies behind.
That friendship's also a fire which burns with gentle light,
That brightens up the darkest day and warms the coldest night.
And glows within a lonely damaged soul,
And makes a broken spirit once more whole.

I have to penetrate your pain
To let your spirit trust again and see
Your heart can yet be free!

Friendship's both the kindling and the fuel
I'll lay within the darkness midst your memories so cruel.
Smothering the ashes from the past,
I'll try to spark a radiant light where shadow now is cast.
But you must set the taper to spread the infant glow,
And slowly feed the growing blaze with all the love you know.
Then let your shining spirit gently start
To warm the waiting passions of your heart.

The light that strains to be released
Once memory's dark power has ceased to reign
Will then be yours again.

Maybe then you'll stand before the hearth,
And think upon the ways you walked, each sad and painful path.
Lost amid the beauty of the flame,
You'll wonder of the reason for the roads by which you came.
For if you'd never suffered deceptions burning brand
You wouldn't be within the warmth
where then you'll quietly stand.
Nor would you feel within your heart the fire
That's kindled from new hope, and from desire.

And should your soul again entrust
Your heart to love that's true and just and right,
You'll never loose that light.

"Only those who will risk going too far can possibly find out how far one can go."
...T. S. Elliot

To Claim the Highest Peak

While traveling alone I saw a distant golden cloud
Upon the highest mountain peak, magnificent and proud.
I wondered at the pinnacle its mists could so enshroud,
So changed my course to see what I might find.
'Twas off on the horizon so I couldn't see it clear.
It felt like half eternity before I'd gotten near.
But still that rugged summit wouldn't let itself appear.
For all I'd see I might as well be blind.

I climbed upon the foothills going steady as I could.
The path I chose was gentle there; the going pretty good,
And each time I would stop to rest I'd look from where I stood,
To see if it was yet within my sight.
But never did my searching eyes reveal that secret fold,
To show to me the mystery I knew those clouds to hold.
And that just fueled my need to know the legends, yet untold,
Of all that could exist at such a height.

The foothills passed below me and the path was getting steep.
The cliffs became more rugged;
the crags became more deep.
But I just kept on climbing to the tryst I had to keep
With all that lay there hidden from my eyes.
At times I'd lose my footing but I'd climb back on the trail.
And times I'd almost fall and feel my spirit start to fail.
Yet always I'd recover as I'd see that mystic veil
Still calling me to claim that waiting prize.

I'd never climbed so high, nor had I ever been so sure,
Nor felt such overwhelming need or energy before.
'Twas when I looked back down to where the eagles quietly soar
I knew that I could reach the goal I sought.
The nearer that I came to what was hidden from my view,
The harder was the climb, and there was nothing that I knew
Could show me from experience the things I'd need to do,
For nothing of this kind was ever taught.

At last I reached a plateau just below the hidden peak.
'Twas surely the most peaceful place on earth a man could seek.
Serenity abounded and my soul could only speak
Of all the mystic beauty that I'd found.
The place was so enchanted that I knew no man but I
Had ever found this magic,
though I'm sure there's some would try.
It's vista reached beyond the range of mankind's mortal eye.
The glow within my heart could not be bound.

If I could do it over it is there I would have stayed.
That plateau offered everything for which I'd ever prayed.
And given without asking that the gift might be repaid;
No other piece of Earth could be so pure.
I chose instead to carry on. To leave that wondrous place
And try to find a way to scale that shrouded mountain face.
I tried to claim its heights as mine; that's where I fell from grace
For no one can that final climb endure.

I see so well in hindsight that no one can claim it all.
For if we seek to climb too high we're always going to fall
To just be left with memories, our dreams that will recall
What could have still been ours if we had stayed.
I glimpsed that wondrous plateau
which no other man was shown,
And should have made it where I am,
not where I once had known,
To walk instead this empty road, now wiser, but alone;
Until this debt of avarice is paid,
And I can be forgiven the mistake
my greed had made:
To crave yet more than heaven
that was once before me laid.

"Only in the agony of parting do we look into the depths of love."
...George Eliot

The Memory of Before

Soft and silently she blows…the warm breeze in the night.
Still and steadily she glows…the old moon shining bright.
Slow and sensuously she flows…the wide sea to the shore.
Sad and solemnly she grows…the memory of before

"Despair is the price one pays for setting oneself an impossible aim."
...Graham Greene

Shattered Dreams

You'll see them abound where marine folk are found
And the dreams of a man turn to sailing.
They're riding the tide while they're trying to hide
That their owner's finances are failing.
They're blistered and bare from the sun's constant glare,
With planking and sails going rotten.
Their ropes are all frayed and their timbers are greyed,
And the ocean is all but forgotten.

Too many's the sailor who gave all he can
To realize all he's been yearning,
To find that his boat, just to keep it afloat,
Costs more than the sum that he's earning.
He scrimps then, and saves, just to stay on the waves
And he'll go without much that he's needing.
And counts not the cost of the lifestyle he's lost
While his future and bank account's bleeding.

His friends though can tell that he's not doing well
As the rails become bare that were varnished.
And the weed grips the keel, and the paint starts to peel,
And the brass round the ports becomes tarnished.
And the rust streaks appear while the 10 a.m. beer
Helps convince him that none of it matters,
Though the dock lines are worn and the sail cover's torn
And the dodger and awning's in tatters.

The dockage comes due but he cannot come through
And he can't pay the annual insurance.
So he anchors outside in the wind and the tide
Where the elements test his endurance.
But the dinghy is soft and the rigging aloft
Needs replacing if he's to go cruising.
And the fuel's almost gone, but he still carries on
Though he knows deep inside that he's losing.

Depression sets in 'neath his stubborn old skin
As he looks at the life that he's squandered.
He won't let it show so that others might know
And he hides the dark thoughts that he's pondered.
He never lets on that his spirit has gone,
Destroyed by his failed ambition
To travel the world with his sails unfurled;
But his friends recognize his condition.

He isn't the first they've see suffer the thirst
For the romance of travelling the oceans.
They've seen them before, wrecked on every shore,
Where the sea can create such emotions.
They seem to abound where marine folk are found
And the dreams of a man turn to sailing.
They're riding the tide of those dreams, now denied,
As their winds all appear to be failing.
They're broken and worn, their hopes now forlorn,
As all of their dreams have turned rotten,
And can't understand why they're back on the land,
And the ocean is all but forgotten.

"It is well to give when asked but it is better to give unasked, through understanding."
... Kahlil Gibran

To Make Love Work

There are many ways to be together,
And every time it's never quite the same.
Some I see from in my past were pretty good, and set to last,
While some were no surprise the ending came.
The outcome always balances on whether
Both support the other's life and dream.
And those that never had a chance
at something more than brief romance
Were when we never worked to be a team.

But still they showed the need to keep on working
To always keep the other's needs to mind.
How energies should freely flow in both directions, come and go.
That love is what you make, not what you find.
And where the traps of love are quietly lurking,
Waiting just to bring another down.
That tolerance is what you need.
More compromise, less selfish greed.
More open smile than disapproving frown.

How energies, if properly united,
Can add to be far greater than the sum.
That two together as a team can realize a far off dream
Where two alone will never see it come.
And why to help the other feel excited
Every time they try for something new.
And how to help achieve their goals,
not fighting to see who controls,
Is what it takes to see a couple through.

And giving them encouragement to try it,
Especially if you can't see why at all.
Telling them you know they can,
and helping them to scheme and plan,
And making sure they rise each time they fall.
And scrimping for what costs too much to buy it,
Nor mentioning the sacrifice you've made.
Nor waiting for a special date to give, so they won't need to wait.
And being their strength whenever they're afraid.

And never asking reasons why they love you,
But telling why you love them so each day.
And showing them how much you care.
And seeking every joy to share,
And listening to each word they want to say.
But never placing them too high above you.
Just being equals trying to share the lead.
Giving in when they should lose,
and asking what they'd like to choose,
Especially when it's not the one you need.

And holding hands when there might be no reason,
Just to let them know you're by their side.
And kissing when they don't know why,
and drying every tear they cry,
And understanding why they might have lied.
And celebrating turnings of the season,
Sharing changes either one may feel.
And trying hard to ease their pain
so you can help them laugh again,
And cleansing every wound that they may heal.

And letting them walk on, if that's their choosing,
To be alone if that's the path they need
To let them have the time and space
to be themselves, to find their place,
To know for sure their spirit yet is freed.
That trapping them you'll only end up losing
Everything you'd hoped to have contained.
That if they should return you'll know
that you were right to let them go,
If not, you'll know they'd never have remained.

For there are many ways to be together,
And every time it's never quite the same.
So learn this from my errant past,
you have to work if love's to last,
Don't treat it like an unimportant game.
The outcome always balances on whether
Both support the other's life and dream.
So if you'd like to have a chance
at something more than brief romance
You have to both make love work as a team.

*"You have brains in your head. You have feet in your shoes.
You can steer yourself in any direction you choose.
You're on your own and you know what you know.
And you are the guy who'll decide where to go."
...Dr. Seuss*

Getting There

If you don't know where you're going
you can't know when you're there.
If you're not sure from where you're leaving
it's doubtful you'll go anywhere.
If you don't care what you want to find
you'll never know where to look.
You'll only find what's left behind
and the roads you wished you took.

To know where you want to be going
you must know what you want to achieve.
You have to establish where you are
to know where you're going to leave.
And you have to know who you want to be
and the person that you have been
Before you can see with clarity the path that lies between.

So cast your eyes to where you are,
not where you'd hoped to be.
And study the roads that leave from there
and check their destiny.
And should you see no roads that run
to where you would end your quest,
Your search is done my wayward son
...you're there
... so stop and rest.

"Sweet is the voice of a sister in the season of sorrow."
...Benjamin Disraeli

The Selkie Son

When the young moon danced on the westing breeze
And the tide was near to spring,
Our bosun stared o'er the silver seas
And soft began to sing.
His song was full of the ebbs and flows
Of lifetimes spent to sail,
And bore strange lore no mortal knows,
In its mythical mystic tale.
And the tune grew slow as the moon grew low
While he sang to the rolling waters.
The stars grew bright in the darkening night
As he sang of his mother's daughters.

In a brogue he sang with many a word
That was only known to the sea.
The rhymes he used had none of us heard
Ever used by another than he.
But none could ever have turned away
While his song was being sung,
As it told of a time where his soul would play
In the realms where he once was young.
And the tune grew slow as the moon grew low
When he sang of enchanted waters.
The tears would rise in his dark sad eyes
As he cried for his mother's daughters.

He sang of the isles of the northern shore
Where folk were of ancient decent.
They lived a life cast in legend and lore
Where the gales would seldom relent.
Where the gull and guillemot side by side
Survived on the weed strewn rocks,
And seal and man both worked the tide
Down the storm battered shores and lochs.
And the tune grew slow as the moon grew low
While he sang of those island waters.
The wind would moan a lament of its own
For the song of his mother's daughters.

He sang of his kin who lived with the sea
From before the islands were old.
With the ancient clan and the seals living free
'Till the days of which legends foretold
When mainland men brought their greed and knives
And destroyed the peaceful days
As they searched for skins of the island wives
And had ended the mystical ways.
And the tune grew slow as the moon grew low
While he sang of the wasteful slaughters
When seal pups cried as their fathers died
Like the cries of his mother's daughters.

We knew the times that his song would begin
By the set of the moon and tide,
And he'd walk to the bow with a leathery skin
Which at all other times he'd hide.
He'd carry it there in his long slender hands
With fingers webbed and strong,
And sing of the past in the mystical lands
Where his clan did once belong.
And the tune grew slow as the moon grew low
While he called far across the waters
To the time when he and the seals swam free
As they played with his mother's daughters.

One midsummer's night we were dodging the rocks
Off a coast that none of us knew.
The full moon reflected from isles and lochs,
When seals began swimming in view.
We crew were fighting so fierce a tide
That I scarce had the time to see
Our bosun climbing down over the side
As he sang his farewell to me.
And his tune grew slow as the moon grew low
While he dived down beneath the waters.
From where he'd gone three grey seals swam on…
… Where they he and his mother's daughters?

"Remorse is the prison of life."
...Charlotte Brontë

I Lost You as a Lover, and a Friend

We really had some good times, you and I.
We reached so many heights it almost seemed as we might fly.
And though the time of romance had to end,
I wish I could be with you, not as lover now, but friend.
For in you lies a beauty to which none can compare,
I've seen it hiding deep inside the heart you tried to share.
It glows within the darkness of your past
Where shadows on its light are cruelly cast.

Yet if I'd known how painful love would be,
The emptiness of loss your soft goodbye has left with me,
I'd chart a different course for us to sail
To bear us to the future on a breeze that wouldn't fail.
For I had loved intensely, and wasn't then aware
That you just needed love that we'd be comfortable to share
That gave each other space in which to live,
And asked much less than I had tried to give.

I knew our ways were different when we met,
Yet thought that was your past that I could help you to forget.
And as you grew to be more than a friend
I looked to where your memories of painful years might end.
And there, within that future, I thought our lives would meld,
I saw your golden glow unfold; the beauty that it held.
And prayed my unbound love would set yours free
To share the joys that both of us could see.

But now I face that future so alone,
I look upon the times we had, the laughter we have known.
As clouds about my pain now slowly clear
I see just how I've cast away the friend I need so near.
For you had seen that future was never meant to be,
And tried in vain to ease my pain as you explained to me,
While I withdrew inside my painful past,
From where my unjust anger then was cast.

And just as all the sorrows that you knew
Had kept from me that part I'd wanted, deep inside of you,
The shadows in the dungeons of my mind
Had hidden at the end your gentle love and left me blind.
And when, so warm and caring, you tried to help me see,
I felt again the years of pain another gave to me,
And blamed you for the years that she had cost,
And tried to make you pay for all I'd lost.

So now I cast reflections on the end
And see that's how I lost not just my lover, but my friend.
And knowing what I never can reclaim,
My heart is cast in sadness and my head is hung in shame.
For you had tried to give me that gift beyond compare,
That wondrous part within your heart you wanted me to share.
To stand, as friend, beside you in the glow
That first had made me love you long ago.

...To stand, as friend, beside you in the glow
That now, my love, I'm never going to know...

"It is well to be up before daybreak, for such habits contribute to health, wealth and wisdom."
...Aristotle

Greeting the New Day in Algonquin

A new day grows each morning, evolving from the past,
Its first grey rays of hope disperse the dark.
My fire glows each dawning from the embers of the last.
A warmth reborn from one surviving spark.

With crystal sunlight flashing in dewdrops of the night
The dawn breeze herds the morning mists away,
The lake shore sets to splashing in silver dappled light
While loon songs cry an anthem to the day.

As nature's unbound beauty adorns the eastern sky
I quietly greet each spirit of the earth,
And recognize my duty to honour, 'till I die,
All life to which the universe gives birth.

Across the hills and ranges, the prairies and the sea,
Each river, every wetland, marsh and lake,
I pray man no more changes this planet, once so free,
And, yet, that he can mend each past mistake.
That, yet, each dawn this glory will still be here for me.
That, yet, each dawn, I'll still be here to wake;
To honour every wonder that mankind needs to be.
To give
And to receive
But not to take.

> *"When one door of happiness closes, another opens, but often we look so long at the closed door that we do not see the one that has been opened for us."*
> *... Helen Keller*

Walk to the Future

Time is too precious to keep looking back
As if there were no tomorrows.
There's just not enough to keep stopping to pack
All your memory's, pains and your sorrows.
Now I've had my hurts, and I've had my despair,
My problems, my losses and strife.
It's not that I'm hard and so no longer care,
I just want to move on with life.
So just 'cos your heart has been broken again,
There's no time to stop here and mope.
Let's cut us a path to the future and then
We can talk of potential and hope.

There is nothing wrong in the feelings you feel.
Nor the yearning for what you now yearn;
But just keep in mind that the past isn't real.
It's gone! It'll never return.
The future's what matters, 'cos that's where you'll be
When love knocks once more at your door.
So better the chances ahead that you see
Than the one's that you missed on before.
'Cos time's way too precious to live in the past
With all the old loves that are done.
So head to the future, and walk pretty fast.
Don't stop 'till the next love's begun.

*"Millions of spiritual creatures walk the earth. Unseen,
both when we wake and when we sleep."*
   ...John Milton

Angels are Keeping

Little one's eyes are frightened and crying.
Life is denying the hope that she'll need.
Onward he tries, her father's defying
The hatred and lying, injustice and greed.

Try not to weep. Look back from your sadness.
See not the badness that brought you these tears.
Go now to sleep in dreams filled with gladness.
Cast out the madness, the pain and the fears.

For you are the one the angels are keeping,
While you lay sleeping they're making you whole.
When this day's done their magic comes creeping
Through tears that you're weeping to brighten your soul.

Cry not my child, your father is hearing,
His courage un-veering with you in his heart.
Loving and mild, he sees all you're fearing,
So paths he is clearing for new hope to start.

Brave then he'll stand unflinching beside you.
A light that will guide you he carries above.
With sword in his hand for those who defied you,
None may deride you so strong in his love.

For you are the one the angels are keeping,
While you lay sleeping they're making you whole.
When this day's done their magic comes creeping
Through tears that you're weeping to brighten your soul.

Dream then of years his battles are ended,
With justice defended and new hope begun.
Gone then the fears as truth will be mended.
Hate apprehended, for love will have won.

Close then this day who's challenges found you,
Tried to surround you with worries and pain.
Let your dreams play where demons can't hound you,
Where daddy has bound you with love once again.

For you are the one the angels are keeping,
While you lay sleeping they're making you whole.
When this day's done their magic comes creeping
Through tears that you're weeping to brighten your soul.

"The teacher who is indeed wise does not bid you to enter the house of his wisdom but rather leads you to the threshold of your mind."
...Kahlil Gibran

The First Tripper

When he joined us that day seems it wasn't the pay
But adventure that he had come seeking.
He was just out of school with the grin of a fool
On a mouth that just couldn't stop speaking
He was willing enough, but he hadn't a clue
Where he should go, what he should do.
And with little idea of the hell you go through
When you sign on to be a first tripper.

On his first day at sea they had sent him to me
For they thought me the best one to teach him.
And it took quite a while for my much older style
To develop a way I could reach him.
And the fact he knew nothing, he wanted to hide,
Partly from fear, partly from pride,
But unlike all the others he never once lied
As a young lad signed on as first tripper.

We were crossing The Bay when I first heard him say
Of his family life he was leaving.
Said his dad was inside, and his mother had died
And he hadn't yet done with his grieving.
Though you'd think he'd no chance
with those cards he'd been dealt,
Not what he said, not what he felt,
He'd just stuck out his chin and he'd tightened his belt
And he'd signed on to be a first tripper.

So I took him in tow to the places we'd go
And I showed him the world he was traveling.
From the dives and the bars, to the planets and stars
As his destiny started unraveling.
It was seventeen months 'till he sailed home again,
Walking with pride, walking with men,
And it's hard to imagine the kid he was when
He'd signed on the crew as first tripper.

Four years went by then before he and I
Sailed again on the same ship together.
She was tired and old and she should have been sold
And we prayed we'd not see any weather.
When a storm over ran us and panicked the crew
He took the wheel. He took us through.
I was proud to be fighting beside him I knew
When I taught him the ropes as first tripper.

When I signed on the ship where I did my last trip
As my tired old bones were complaining,
Was the pride of the sea that they'd offered to me
For to finish my time still remaining.
As I walked up the gangway the Captain I spied.
Ran to the bridge! Ran to his side!
And I couldn't help crying the tears that I cried,
When I realized just who was the skipper.
And it fills up an old sailors heart full of pride
Knowing he was who taught that first tripper.

"Two things are infinite: the universe and human stupidity; and I'm not so sure about the universe."
...Albert Einstein

Letting the Universe Guide my Way.

I traveled all my life to places most will never know.
And been a hundred different roads and seen all they could show,
But this here's yet the strangest road down which I'll ever go.
And I don't have a clue where it might lead.
It took a load of courage for a man who's not so strong
To recognize the ways I've lived my life, 'till now, are wrong.
'Cos when I saw in retrospect the roads I walked along,
I realized those paths were picked by greed.

I don't know where I'm going, I just know I have to get,
For every place I've been sure hasn't been the right one yet.
Don't ask of me what path I'll take, or course that I might set.
I don't know where I'll be once I am gone.
It sounds a little crazy, but I know I'll be okay,
'Cos now the Universe is going to mark for me the way
That leads from here to someplace where
my conscience lets me stay.
I trust Her choice of roads to walk upon.

It isn't that I'm stupid if you look at what man's done,
We've been here such a little while beneath this ancient sun
Yet screwed up every blessed thing that Nature had begun,
While She just quietly watched and understood.
She knew we'd soon be come and gone with hardly any trace.
And once we'd left She'd just repair our damage to this place
And carry on regardless like She never saw our face,
While everything unfolds the way it should.

To her we're nothing more than Krakatau at full blast.
We come on like a steam train and destroy the living past
And change this world we live in with our ego, blind and vast,
And think we are the masters of our realm.
Well that's not how I see it 'cos I know now that's not true.
We're nothing but a parasite with nothing else to do
But try to suck out resources this planet can't renew.
The Universe, not us, is at the helm.

She's steering us so straight and true upon some leeward shore
With wind and tide now gathering like never once before
To break us on the rocks of nature's unforgiving law;
...Don't ever take out more than you can give...
She's seen all we've been taking, and I guess has had her fill,
And any day we're going to feel the sharp edge of her will,
And, don't forget, She wrote the book on what and why to kill,
And when it's best for something not to live.

I could have stayed to spend my life like any other man,
Just taking and not giving, 'cos he reckons that he can.
But now I've seen that has no place in Nature's master plan
I want Her now to guide my errant way.
And it's not only me that's seen our future's not secure.
There's thousands more across the earth
that knows we can't endure.
Unless we change our attitude, we're history, for sure,
And mankind will have surely had its day.

And, just like every other thing, we screwed *that* up as well.
We've contributed nothing good, as far as I can tell,
Yet taken all we wanted, and so made of Eden Hell;
Destroying all we did, or didn't, need.
So I'm not being crazy as I leave my past behind
To trust the Universe to show what future I might find.
I'd rather follow hers than any plan of humankind
To seek a life of balance not of greed.

So here I bid my fond farewells to those of you that stay.
It's been a real pleasure, but I'd best be on my way.
I hope to see you someplace, on some other happy day
When you decide to reconcile your fate.
I'm off to let the Universe show what She has in store,
And teach me how to take much less,
while giving so much more.
That is if She'll accept me after all I've done before.
I hope I haven't found this road too late…

"The hottest love has the coldest end."
...Socrates

Winter of a Broken Heart

Frost on his mouth stretched gaunt by the storm,
Hands thrust in pockets beside him.
Thinking of days which would ever be warm
Back in the isles now denied him.
Narrowing shoulders he bends to the breeze,
Tightening his jacket around him.
Hating this land so remote from the seas,
Here where misfortune has bound him.

Snow lashes sharply his tropical eyes.
Chill cuts a shiver right through him.
Set is the sun from eternal blue skies,
Lost, like the woman that knew him.
Cast now his life to this northerly cold
Far from the islands which bore him.
Come is his fate that was never foretold
Borne on the winter before him.

Frozen, his tears set to ice on his cheeks,
Track where his memories placed him,
Far from the warmth and the love that he seeks.
Damned where his destiny faced him.
Here where his heart met its final reward,
Cursed where his penance now binds him
Ever to ask why his love was ignored.
Gone where no solace can find him.

"The river has taught me to listen; you will learn from it, too. The river knows everything; one can learn everything from it."

...Herman Hesse (Siddhartha)

River of my Sussex Childhood

River of my Sussex childhood, ebb and flow inside of me
From your birth in Wealden wild wood to the all accepting sea.
Long I trekked your banks of chalk
to share my dreams, my pain and fears
With you, with whom I chose to talk
amid those young tempestuous years.

Wise were you beyond perception, teaching me the ways to see.
Well you taught of introspection, understanding first...the me.
Then, through natures take-and-giving,
showed you me the balanced ways,
Loss and gain, from which my living
creed has borne me all these days.

Life was there with all its glory,
showing me each purpose planned,
Saw I too in every story
nature's wild and quiet command.
There with you I learned to borrow only that for which I'd need.
Then return it on the morrow…Harvest not what I can't seed.

There I learned that where I passed
I'd leave each place as it was found,
Give life first and take it last. Gently tread upon the ground.
Find the spoor and, quiet, come near
the timid lives I'd wish to see,
Or pass another creature clear whose life I'd put in jeopardy.

Then you taught me well the learning
still which strengthens me this day,
Tides are constant in their turning,
lows and highs can never stay.
Just when hope seems drained of reason,
quietly then the floods begin.
Gently turns another season. Then to lose, but now to win.

From your banks I learned of beauty,
heard the natural rhythms pound.
Touched the thread through which, by duty,
every mortal form is bound.
Saw the purpose of existence, understood the rite of death.
Studied nature's quiet persistence.
Smelled the scent of freedom's breath.

There I learned of pride, and pity, joy and sorrow, loss and gain.
Now, within this stagnant city, still I feel you flow again.
You're still in my veins and virtue.
You're still in my trust and truth.
My respect will not desert you. It's still there, as in my youth.

Still you ebb and flow inside me, cleansing out this city's grime.
Strong and true your currents guide me on toward a better time.
Though this day is filled with sorrow.
Though this night is filled with pain.
Dawn shall bring a new tomorrow. Tides shall ever turn again.

Nothing ever lasts forever, save the path of destiny.
Though it tries, this city never shall destroy the best in me.
For that's you, oh gentle river. That is you who taught me so.
That is you, my solace giver. Bear me wither I may go.

"The way of paradoxes is the way of truth."
...Oscar Wilde

Love's Paradox

Me strong suit ain't philosophy, but thinkin's been me way,
Especially when it comes to gettin' burned.
I 'aven't told no-one but me the things me mind will say,
But now it seems there's much what I 'ave learned.
So 'ere I'm gonna share wiv you a gift that cost me dear
In all the pain it took to be self-taught.
So open up an ear or two, an' pull that chair up near
So's you can understand the clever things what I 'ave thought.

I've 'ad me several lovings start, an' all 'ave ended wrong.
Seemed one or other of us couldn't last.
It's been so when I shares me 'eart me partners don't stay long,
They all become enigmas of me past.
An' now that I'm an older bloke, in wisdom, not just age,
I think I've worked out why I'm still alone.
The reason why me heart gets broke on every bleedin' page
Is down to this 'ere paradox me mind to me has shown.

You see we live instinctively, and everyone's the same
When looking at each simple basic need,
Of which there's two, conflictingly, when factored in the game,
Where love's potential problems spawn and breed.
The one tells us to curl up snug in someone else's strength,
All wrapped in warmth an' comfort, love an' grace.
The other, an' now here's the bug, will go to any length
To keep our independence so's our ego stays in place.

And there's the damn confoundedness, I sees it clear an' plain,
That sabotages all me tries at love.
For 'though I needs 'er warm caress, that's just what causes pain
Right where me id and ego push an' shove.
Right when I'm feelin' safe an' sound a-sharin' of 'er life,
An' lovin' every second we're as one,
Me independence takes the ground and gives me holy strife
By yellin' that, to stay as me, I'd better bloody run!

No wonder me philanderin' so often doesn't hold,
An' always leaves me guessin' what went wrong.
Me feelin's keep meanderin' 'tween hot and bleedin' cold,
Enough to foil the weak and fool the strong.
It ain't just me that's torn this way, 'tween solo and duet,
'Twixt company, an' comfort on me own.
It's everyone, I have to say, that I have ever met
Who's trapped between a need to be, yet fear of being, alone.

So now I've found what's buggin' me in matters of the 'eart.
I understands this syndrome of the self.
The choice is not 'tween "I" or "we", or should I stop or start.
Nor is it 'tween the altar and the shelf.
The choice is in the one I choose, an' how I then be'ave
If love's not going to vanish into doubt.
'Cos all that's there that I might lose, I just as might could save
If only I could cast some basic common sense about.

So next time that I find for me a lass who'll take me 'and
I'll slow it down and spend time on me own,
An' watch the way she acts to see if she might understand
There's times as I might want to be alone.
An' if she lets me stroll away whenever I might need
An' always lets me walk back when I'm done,
An' never need to fear the day me freedom might recede
An' never think it's time I ought to turn me tail an' run.
Then probably I've found for me an end to all me pain;
The one who's arms I'll never need to leave.
Cos', long as I can still feel free I might as well remain
Where id and ego, side by side, love's paradox deceive.

"I would rather wake up in the middle of nowhere than in any city on earth."
...Steve McQueen

The City

I've lived among fighters and sensed what they fear.
Learned how it feels knowing death might be near.
And found a friend's corpse while I choked back a tear.
But I never felt threatened 'till I landed here.

I've been through some hurricanes, fought them and won.
Trekked through the wild lands so glad for my gun.
Took fever so bad I thought life was but done.
But never, 'till now, had I wanted to run.

I took all the slandering, still I stood tall.
And stared at defeat, but I never would fall.
Been battered and bloodied, yet answered the call.
But here I feel ready to give up, and crawl.

Those fears and the hardships, the tears and the pain,
Are only what forces of nature ordain.
So I'm glad to have known them and all they sustain.
But I can't take this city
This sanitized city
Where nothing that's natural could ever remain.

"Freedom is not a matter of choice, it is a destined path, an undying yearning for the peace of one's soul until attainment."
...Sir Winston Churchill

The Lake

Of all the times I've walked beside you never once I understood,
Nor even when I sailed upon your surface, grey and coldly bleak.
I criticized and disrespected, seeing just what wasn't good
And thought you an imposter for the ocean that I ever seek.

Upon your tortured soul I laid
the blame borne of my longing heart
That yearned for open waters
and the freedom that they quietly know.
I neither looked for comradeship
or solace from our troubled start,
Desiring our relationship be destined not to further grow.

Now, after nearly four long years of never giving you a chance
I find, like an epiphany, that we are nothing but the same.
Both locked by land where nary an adventure, nor a true romance
Is ours to even contemplate, nor ever yet to try to claim.

As me, you're fed from many spirits
each born from a different source,
That join and swell in flowing turmoil onward to your aching heart.
There to stay, imprisoned by the shores
through which you cannot force
A passage to the sea of which you'd love so much to be a part.

You and I are desperate brethren,
caged within un-chosen bounds.
Captive in an unforgiving place where neither one should be.
One day, though, I shall escape
this cursed land that now surrounds
Us both, and, unlike you, my landlocked friend,
that day I'll reach the sea.

"Where did we come from? What are we doing here? Is there meaning or purpose to our existence? Do we have a soul? What happens to us after we die?"
...Deepak Chopra

Quest for the reason

For nigh on eighty years we'll live upon this blessed earth.
Not once will life decide to give the reason for our birth.
From innocence we grow to ask the endless question, "Why
Has nature made our life long task appear to be to die?"

Small difference are our lives to make on those to yet be born.
No claim to greatness may we stake. No halos to adorn
These modest heads, which sought the truth
and so turned every stone
From early days of questing youth to dying, then, alone.

Not one of us can truly say "'Twas I that changed this world."
Though some may loose such dreams to play
as banners are unfurled
To celebrate a noble thought, immortalize a deed;
Their single efforts were of naught.
Their claim to fame but greed.

For they were merely part of all that happened to that day.
'Twas they but claimed the champion's call before the final fray,
By boasting theirs to be the plan which journeyed from before
The dawning of the time of man; that's yet to journey more.

For they were but a speck in time who, accidentally thrust
By circumstance, were seen to climb from evolution's dust.
Borne on and up by deeds of those who never were to know
Their part in all that history shows, and where it yet will go.

As countless ants we've scurried though
our lives, from dawn to death.
To add, with all we think and do from first to final breath,
To destinies we'll never see, for reasons we can't guess.
Accepting this futility. Embracing pointlessness.

For though we sing and statues raise for those we laud as great,
Their contribution earns no praise in history's debate.
Remembered for a thousand years,
a speck they've still remained,
For when eternal memory clears, such claims are not sustained.

Both meek and mighty each in turn must serve a greater need
Who's reason man has yet to learn, no matter what his creed.
As atoms in the cosmos we are infinitely small,
And understand just what we see, and see not much at all.

For nigh on eighty years we'll live upon this blessed earth.
And never once will history give a reason to our birth.
From innocence we'll grow and ask the endless question, "Why
Does nature make our life long task appear to be to die?"
From innocence we've grown to ask the
endless question, "Why?"
…To seek that answer is our task,
…eternally to try.

"Knowest thou not the beauty of thine own face? Quit this temper that leads thee to war with thyself."
... Jalal ad-Din Rumi

A Daughter At Rest

Asleep, she lies at peace.
The tears and tantrums cease
And all is quiet within her world, and calm.
Adrift amid her dreams;
Slow breaths replacing screams.
The devils rest while angels guard from harm.

Her hair on cushions spread
A halo round her head
Or so it's seemed whenever she has slept.
A shadow on her eyes
Just helps to emphasize
The depths from where ten minutes past she wept.

A smile adorns her face
With solace out of place
About this infant tempest of before.
Someone who'd never seen
Would swear she's never been
Such maelstrom, nor could she yet be more.

But more she'll surely be
Her ambiguity
Will rise again to keep us all confused.
One minute laughter filled,
The next she's demon willed
Then back to one contented and amused.

But, truly, at her worst,
When sanity's reversed,
Her temper isn't really hell inspired.
Compared to some, she's mild;
A tranquil, easy child
Whose patience shows erosion when she's tired.

That's why she's sleeping so.
Though just a while ago
You may have thought a Dervish was abroad!
A rest was overdue.
Her patience went askew
And left her gentle nature somewhat flawed.

But now she lies at peace.
The tears and tantrums cease,
And all is quiet within her world of sleep.
Adrift within her dreams.
For now, no shrieks and screams.
The devils gone as angels watch and keep.
And smiling, wet-eyed Fathers quietly peep
And unashamed accept their turn to weep.

"It always seems impossible until it is done."
...Nelson Mandela

To Reach the Distant Summit.

Straining weary, watery eyes
To where horizons meet the skies
I stare upon a mountain's lonely peak.
And though the road ahead is gone,
I've vowed to ever journey on
To reach that distant summit that I seek.

Though pain I know awaits me there
Should I once chance, with absent care,
To leave the hidden pathways I must tread.
Yet, small the progress I might make,
With every cautious step I take
I near that mystic mountain up ahead.

And though, by many varied roads
I've borne such huge and heavy loads,
There's nothing I have brought can help me now.
No trails that I have walked upon
Compare with this, but, right or wrong,
I'll strive to reach that peak, though God knows how.
I'll strive to reach that icy peak,
However tired. However weak.
As long as my endurance will allow.

"And one by one the nights between our separated cities
are joined to the night that unites us."
...Pablo Neruda

Separation

Never a day I didn't pause
Amid the most engrossing things,
To search for you amid the wars
Of doubt which separation brings.
Never a night I didn't turn
And breath a soft, abandoned, moan,
And pray to God that I could learn
If you, like I, were still alone.
Never an hour I didn't miss
That gentle touch, that whispered word,
That unexpected, unsought, kiss,
That solemn phrase just barely heard.

"A smile is the chosen vehicle of all ambiguities."
...Herman Melville

Behind the Smile

Still memories of sorrows hid within your smile
Through dreams of your tomorrows linger for a while,
Remembering those tragic years
When came the pain, when came the tears
And sadness quietly took your empty hand.
A time life lost its laughter. Faith became unsure.
You feared what might come after the loss you'd need endure.
You'd trusted through the eyes of youth,
So unprepared when painful truth
Destroyed that trust you'd come to understand.

Dreams were tossed and shattered. Anger filled your heart.
Much of all that mattered crashed and broke apart.
You had to turn in vengeful spite
To slake the thirst to hate, to fight.
You had to strike the one who gave such pain.
And selfishly defending all you knew was lost,
You recognized the ending but couldn't see the cost,
So fought with every blade you'd find,
With every word that came to mind,
But when the fight was done what did you gain?

Broken then, and bleeding, you searched about your life
To find where it was leading. A devastated wife
You cried into your empty hands
And prayed to Him who understands
To help your damaged spirit to sustain.
Then, thinking as a mother, you turned from what had died.
From one hurt and another you dragged your broken pride
And put behind the things he'd done.
You turned from where the pain begun,
And from the loss you built your lives again.

How slow those days were numbered, climbing to the light.
So heavily encumbered by all that wasn't right.
You bore the silent weight of grief
And found inside your lost belief
That you were worthy. You'd succeed once more.
Children warm beside you, youth still close to hand,
Despite the tears you cried you dreamed
and schemed and planned
And came toward this very day
Where now you fill my eyes and say
"I'm here. It matters not what went before."

But still I see that sorrow hid within your smile.
Your dreams about tomorrow falter for a while
Amid the thoughts of where you've been,
The pain and trials your soul has seen,
The tears you've cried through all you've had to bear.
I see in you another, scarred from loss and pain,
D'you see in me a brother who seeks his soul again?
D'you see in me a shattered heart
Too scared to beat, too scared to start
Toward that point where once more it may share?

I've felt those same emotions. Seen the grief you've seen.
Shared the same devotions for those caught in between.
I understand that fearful cost
Of just how much of you is lost
When love is turned to hate and pain and lies.
I offer then my shoulder to help you bear your past.
I see, now I am older, how destinies are cast,
And offer you my open mind
Where others, younger, may be blind
Not having seen your pain through sorrowed eyes.

I watch where you've created from all the hurt you've felt
A love where once you hated, a light where dark once dwelt.
A home where children grow and thrive,
And happiness is yet alive.
Where words are kind and discipline is just.
Yet feel your soul still trying, despite the tears you wept,
To understand the lying and pains it can't accept,
So offer all I have to give
To help your faith in others live …
…An honest quiet friendship you can trust.

And hope this might diminish the past within your smile,
That reticence may finish and doubting reconcile.
And hope that if your soul can learn
It yet may trust…that in it's turn
My soul may learn from yours, and also mend.
But 'til that day *my* sorrows may ride within *my* smile.
Though dreams of new tomorrows may linger for a while
Where sadness holds *my* empty hand
And keeps *me* from the dreams *I've* planed…
…And keeps *me* scared to trust an honest friend.

"Do not judge, and you will never be mistaken."
...Jean-Jacques Rousseau

Of Thylkes and Frumps

A drumpling frump one summer's day
came grimbling through the wood,
I wished him well upon his way and offered him some food.
He scoffed and scringed and skrinkled up
to where I'd made my camp,
And cleared my plate and drained my cup
and started then to stamp.

"Silly the man who friendship gives!
"Stupid who shares his dinner!
"Better to frump, like how I lives
"And always be the winner."

He grimbled off and soon was gone, though still I heard his voice
So loud he gluffed and gudgled on, I hadn't any choice.
So when at last the forest stilled, and snoodgers gently groled,
I cursed and frilled and stingly trilled and frumpies I did scold.

"Lucky the one who lends a hand.
"Happy who helps another.
"Pity who'll never understand
"That every lad's his brother."

Right there before my biglid eyes as bright as any plimp
A full grown thylke stood twice the size
of half a snockled shrimp.
Though thrice by half at least his weight,
he'd washed and dried my cup
And somehow heftyhobbed the plate
and cleaned the draggots up.

"Merry the one who shares the chores.
"Joyful the hard earned blister.
"Pity the one whose mind ignores
"That every gal's his sister."

I'd only ever readed thylkes in librerarely books
I'd seen some squebs and grottywhilks
so knew just how they looks.
But thylkes, now they was something more
from other lands than here.
I scratched me nog and squitched me jaw
and squbbed me ruttled ear,

"Lucky the chap who meets a thylke,
"Blissed the bloke that sees 'im.
"Would 'e like crumps, or glugs o' milk?
"How then may I please 'im?"

At that his eyes lit up with glee. He danced a merry jiggle,
And hopped and bopped right up to me and chortlingly did giggle.
He scrumped and jumped, and clumped and bumped
and danced his thylkie dance,
Then on a log he grandly plumped and gave a grimbling glance.

"Pleases me when a friend of thylke
"Asks thylke to share his eatings.
"Don't need no crumps or glugs o' milk.
"Just need your friendly greetings."

With that he upped and flashed and sparked
and sploophed from where I'd seen him
Where not a trottled foot-print marked;
could that have really been him?
I searched and sought and tredged in thought
that maybe I had dozed
And dreamed him there as really naught
that's real, but just supposed.

"Thought I had left my thriffelled friend?
"Thought I had gone without you?
"Never a thylke would bring to end
"A lesson that's about you."

He hung upside a downward tree and grinned a knowing winker
And changed there right in front of me
from thylke to frumpy tinker.
Then back to thylke he changed again,
then back to frump he travelled.
Not just as one would he remain, but
twain, entwined and ravelled.

"Chose you to like the chortling one.
"Chose you to scold the other.
"Didn't you know when all is done
"They both from singling mother."

And then I knewed what he did said although he hadn't word it.
He'd slinked a think inside my head as good as if I'd heard it.
In every chump there's thylke and frump;
'cos everyone's a double.
We're smile and grump, we're svelte and plump,
we're goodie-good and trouble.

"So better not scold the frump you see
"And base on that your thoughtlings.
"Better to wait 'cos they might be
"A thylke abust with chortlings.

"Better not haste to primly judge
"Based on a first formed greetings.
"Better to wait to wear a grudge
"'Till subsequential meetings."

"'Cos lucky the chap who meets a thylke,
"Blissed the bloke can reach him,
"Speshley when met as frumpish ilk
"That grimbled there to teach him."

"Almost all of our sorrows spring out of our relationships with other people."
...Arthur Schopenhauer

Choose Well

Choose well, my love, the one who may
Replace me in your heart.
Choose carefully for you could slay
That small remaining part
Of faith I used to have in love
Surviving deep inside.
Choose well the man you place above
Your love for me that died.

"We are tied to the ocean. And when we go back to the sea, whether it is to sail or to watch - we are going back from whence we came."
... John F. Kennedy

Over the Ocean

Of the places I've been and the countries I've seen
There are none that I'd choose over sailing.
When we've anchors aweigh on a fresh winters day
And we're catching the winds now prevailing,
I'd be up on the main yards unlashing the sails,
Searching the seas, searching the breeze,
With me weathered eye looking for signs of the gales
That'll carry me over the ocean.

Underneath a new moon in a quiet lagoon
With the palms in the wind gently swaying.
It's peaceful and still, but it drains a man's will
For the work for which owners are paying
When I'm furling the tops'ls ahead of the squall,
Lashed by the rain, lashed by the pain,
I'll be laughing aloud while I'm risking it all
'Cos I'm running free over the ocean.

With the harbour town nights winking out their delights
From the lassies who want to come find me.
It's a rum run ashore, and I've been there before,
Now I'm glad that those days are behind me.
It's the plunge of the bowsprit that ploughs through the waves,
Calls me to go, calls me to know
It's the challenge of nature my wandering heart craves
That I find sailing over the ocean.

Near the small island town, where my mother's laid down,
There's a cottage that's mine for the taking.
And there's work on the farm where I'll come to no harm
For the earnings that's there for the making.
But the pitch of the mizzen while working aloft,
Straining to fold, straining to hold,
Is for me more rewarding than working that croft
Where you can but look over the ocean.

So don't ask me why I don't give it a try,
On the land where my family came from.
I'm a sailor you see, Callum Stuart, that's me,
And my kin's just where I got that name from.
There all likeness was ended and ties were undone.
Sailed from the shore, sailed home no more.
I'm the black sheep, the rebel, the prodigal son,
Who went sailing out over the ocean.

When my life is all through, this I'm asking o' you
That no matter the place that I'm laying,
You must bear me to sea, where the wind's blowing free
And the selkie and kittywake's playing.
In the roughest of waters just heave me below,
Lashed in a sail, lashed by the gale,
And then cast in your flowers and leave them to flow
In the wind and tide over the ocean.
So my spirit may sail where eternal gales blow
While me soul may glide over the ocean.

"They that go feel not the pain of parting; it is they who stay behind that suffer."
...Henry Wadsworth Longfellow

'Twas Good While It Lasted

Good bye my old girl, 'twas good while it lasted.
We made a great pair for the time that we had.
I'm sorry it turned out that I'd be the bastard
Who'd leave when I felt those good times turning bad.
And though I'd look back to the fun that we'd make,
(And we made quite a load while the good times were there)
I still, when those good times were all in our wake,
Just had to move on, though I didn't know where.

Those good times were great though. No question of sadness,
No thoughts of tomorrow, just living for now.
But where did they go girl? From where came that badness?
And why did they leave us? And just when and how?
'Cos I never wanted those good times to stop,
And I know you were loving those times we would live.
I guess life can't let us stay there at the top
After living so fast all the fun it can give.

I guess we just used up a ton of resources
And crammed them exhausted in one little space.
But who looks at fate when the natural forces
Of love spur you on, 'till you meet face to face?
And then it's too late to rethink all you've done
And go back and try starting over again.
But if we'd known that when our travels begun
We might not have started what we started then.

There's no way to know, so let's not ask questions.
But best to accept things the way that they are.
Best not to glance at those wistful reflections
Of what might have been now we've both come too far.

Best to just say that we both had life mastered
When thinking of times back when nothing was bad.
Then say to ourselves 'twas good while it lasted.
We made a great pair for the time that we had.

"Beauty is the greatest seducer of man."
...Paulo Coelho

Okavango

I search for her in magazines and T.V. shows,
And talk of her whenever there is someone there she knows.
And even though she's seldom any place which I can find,
I always see her vision in my mind.

Okavango!
Though she has never heard my name
Since first I heard hers spoken my life's never been the same.
Though many thousand miles from where
she's dancing through the sand,
I dream that we were dancing hand in hand.

Although I've never been to where I know she lives,
I feel the rare excitement that her wondrous presence gives.
For other men have told me of their sojourns at her side,
And all the savage beauty she can hide.

Okavango!
Her distant magic sometimes heard,
Borne far across the oceans by that single mystic word.
But how can such enchantment in this modern age exist?
And why am I so helpless to resist?

I tried to reach her desert realm in years gone by
But wilderness and war then blocked the paths I chose to try.
And though the thought of failure weighed
my younger heart with pain,
It bred mature resolve to try again.

Okavango!
Though she could not have known of me,
If I never see another, she is one sight I must see.
Elusiveness and distance now just fuel the raging fire
That burns my longing spirit with desire.
She calls to me at night when I can't fall asleep.
She tempts me with her sirens' songs of secrets that she'll keep
Until the day I go to where her hidden pleasure lies,
To feast upon her beauty with my eyes.

Okavango!
Our souls must one day intertwine.
But should I die before the time that honour has been mine,
I'll leave this life content my dying heart still bears her name,
To seek her in my next life just the same.

"A ruffled mind makes a restless pillow."
...Charlotte Brontë

Thoughts at Four in the Morning

I hope she doesn't wake at night to quietly speak my name
And wonder if I'm missing her beside me, just the same.
But if she should, I pray to God she'll know she bears no blame
For reasons why we both now sleep alone.
I hope she doesn't stare upon that silent empty space
Beside her on the pillow where she once caressed my face.
Nor try to snuggle close to feel the warmth of my embrace,
Remembering the nights that we had known.

I hope she doesn't reminisce to days we used to share,
Each time she sees a candle flame, and feels that I'm not there.
But if she does, I pray she'll know I'm always going to care
Though now we both must live our days apart.
I hope she doesn't mourn the loss of beauty that has died,
And wipe away a silent tear that flows from deep inside.
Or wonder if her memories of love will be denied,
For she still lives within my aching heart.

For though I'd love the times we knew to be ours once again,
I know it can't be so, and this is how we must remain.
And so I pray she'll never feel the sorrow or the pain
I've carried deep inside me since the end.
But if she knows this sadness, and so feels the way I feel,
Then she will also know the love we had was surely real,
And one day, maybe soon, that love I tore apart may heal,
'Till I can stand beside her as a friend.

And one day, maybe soon, these sleepless nights may yet reveal
This aching heart, now broken, yet can mend.

"All of life is a foreign country."
...Jack Kerouac

In Search of Home

Where is my home? I have no true notion,
Living this long so far and so wide
Where journey's have steered me through every ocean
To ride on each current and wait on each tide.
If home were defined where ones time is spent longest,
Mine would be shaded by tropical palms.
Or if it should be where the calling is strongest,
Mine's the savanna's primordial charms.
Or would it be found where one's children are playing,
Mine would be subject to seasons of freeze.
Or where errant memories often go straying,
Mine would be sailing free over the seas.

Where is my home? There's the confusion.
Neither a house nor a dwelling I own.
I live in this city, but that's an illusion.
Home cannot be where one feels so alone.
Leaving the places of manhood and duty,
Maybe my home should be where I was grown.
The banks of a river. A peace, and a beauty.
A church and a farm yard. A house I had known.
A village school, lambing field, paddock and fishing,
Thatch on the roof tops and Sussex flint walls.
The black "Steyning Stinker" all puffing and swishing.
These are but some of what childhood recalls.

Can home be so, as memory knowing
How life then once used to be so long ago?
Surely one's home must be one that is showing
A present reality. Somewhere you know.
I am no more of the boy who once wandered
O'er every acre that estuary held.
I'm of the man with a life that was squandered
To ocean and mountain, island and veldt.
Gone is the youth to whom that home was speaking,
Deafened by years of adventure abroad.
Grown is the man with the quest he's been seeking
With sextant and fountain pen, plough share and sword.

What of that quest, and what of those travels,
And what is this grail I've so stubbornly sought?
Now that, with age, youths reason unravels,
Has it been worth all the battles I've fought?
Can it now justify life's deprivations
Littering every road that I took?
Will it sustain a man's aspirations
Who knew not his future, but wanted to look?
Could it be so that the dream I'm pursuing,
Forcing me ever, and further, to roam,
Is merely a hope that I'll find, by so doing,
A place I can rest where my soul may call home?
Could it then be that I've traveled for ever
Searching for that which I once knew so well?
Losing it then, now fearing I'm never
To find me another home this side of hell?

"Nothing is so commonplace as to wish to be remarkable."
...William Shakespeare

The Walters and I

(Thoughts of the Sir Walters Scott and Raleigh)

Would that I'd write what my heart wants to say
In verses whose theme's wouldn't falter.
Or Sail a ship bound discovery's way
To Nassau, Barbados, Gibraltar.
Be granted a knighthood by Queens of the day
For poems or deeds that exalt her.
Instead of just dreaming this morning away
Of Sir Walter, myself, and Sir Walter.

It's not such an idle dream lying with me,
Though doubtful I'll ever be knighted.
Like Raleigh, I've spent many years on the sea;
Like Scott, long in rhyme I've delighted.
But now I'm outside of the Queens sovereignty
In isles that with palm trees are blighted,
I fear my poor deeds and my poor poetry
Would leave Wally and Wally quite frighted!

"We may have found a cure for most evils; but we have found no remedy for the worst of them all, the apathy of human beings."
   ...Helen Keller

Epitaph

No stone has he on which to carve these lines.
Below the ocean's surface lies his grave
In dappled shadows turning all that shines
To half forgotten memories with every passing wave.

He's resting much the same as he would live,
Where random currents moved him to and fro'.
Accepting the directions they would give
To travel where their wayward wills would have his spirit go.

So landed he a life upon the sea,
Adrift amidst the notions of the tides.
Mistaking aimlessness for being free.
Ambitions for horizons which the distance always hides.

And now his head is lain amongst the weed
Where still he worries not for where he goes.
So innocent of coveting or greed,
Content, his soul will walk whichever path St. Peter chose.

And should he find there Satan and his fire,
He'll surely be rejected from that place.
For never did he own a strong desire.
And never made a willful move that ended in disgrace.

Yet should that path lead upward to the light,
Lord Gabriel will surely turn him back.
Though nothing wrong, his life showed nothing right
By which he could be qualified to sail on heaven's tack.

Immortal spirit, like his mortal soul,
Now doomed to sail the penitential sea,
Between the shores of wasted lives will roll,
Eternally adrift aboard the ship of apathy.

"Who sows virtue reaps honour."
...Leonardo da Vinci

Wake Well This Day

Wake to this dawn like no day before you.
Rise to this morning like no other morn.
Night is now past and life can't ignore you.
Feel in the sunrise your future be born.

Seek every trail the new light may show you.
Open your mind to each challenging thought.
Search for the goodness in those who would know you.
Harness the hope that the new day has brought.

Live well each hour this dawn will afford you,
Use well each minute to honour your soul.
Earn every gift with which life can reward you.
Turn every dream to a meaningful goal.

Smile as each innocent beauty will find you.
Laugh at the ugliness cast in your way.
Break free from memory's chains that would bind you.
Hate not the past and so love for today.

Wake then to live by your spirit and virtue.
Hold every moment and thought to your heart.
Know then that laughter and love won't desert you,
Both will be yours ere this day will depart.

Wake then this dawn with angels to guide you.
Rise to this morning like none you have known.
Sleep then this night with love close beside you.
No more to wake to your future, alone.

"Honour means that a man is not exceptional; fame, that he is. Fame is something which must be won; honour, only something which must not be lost."
...Arthur Schopenhauer

An Ordinary Man

There'll be no portrait hanging on the walls
Of institutions honouring the great,
Displaying, semi-profile, in their halls
My regal stance and posture, and my much ennobled state.

There'll be no volumes lined upon the shelves
Of academics, experts in their field,
From which they'll take my words to use themselves
And praise their contribution and the wisdom that they yield.

Nor lands and seas that bear my famous name
So given for the man who dared to find,
And, for his God and country, laid his claim
That both could spread their influence, and fortune, if inclined.

No, just a barren cross and pile of stone
Is all there'll be to mark this life I led.
A man who came and went his way alone.
Not great, nor wise or famous.
Just a good man who's now dead.

Afterword

My interest in the writing of poems is largely due to my Father who, when I was yet quite young, instilled a wonder for the art by reciting some of the greatest lyrical verse, often without need of written text before him, while we sat digesting my Mother's delicious Sunday lunches. He would not just recite them but help me experience them; feel how their rhythm could add perspective to their canvas, as in Robert Browning's *'How They Brought the Good News from Ghent to Aix'* where the cadence of each line carries the tempo of galloping horses; explain the social importance of them through the example of Rudyard Kipling's *'Barrack Room Ballads'* by which excellent poetry was removed from the private domain of the educated upper classes and made available in a format the general public could enjoy; envision epic historical events through works such as Thomas Babington Macaulay's *'How Horatius Kept the Bridge'* where heroic acts were vividly depicted against the vast backdrop of the Roman Empire.

If there was one influence that was to truly set me on the course of writing my own verse it was my Father's writing of his. By so sharing his own work with me he showed that the skill was surely accessible to anyone who wanted to try, and they didn't have to have witnessed heroic deeds, been a great philosopher or travelled to the ends of the earth to do so; although perhaps the poem of my Father's that stands out most in my mind actually does incorporate elements of all three of those stimuli. It is based not about heroes or philosophy, but about one of the humblest of occurrences that took place during my Father's six year participation in World War Two. That in itself was yet another lesson in the poet's art for me; that there are worthy subjects to be found everywhere you look, even in apparently mundane events, if you do but look.

So to close this book of my own work I am going to pay tribute to the only poetry teacher I have ever known; a man who would be considered by scholars unworthy of that task, but a man who, in the reality of life as I've learned to understand it, was probably more qualified than most scholars I have met. Here is my father's poem to a war time comrade with whom he fought side by side through many hard won battles, travelled thousands of miles through many foreign lands, watched mutual friends fall, and together celebrated when the war was won, the carnage ended and they could go home to London and pick up their old lives where they had left them behind so many years before. The poem though is about none of those poignant and emotional scenarios. Instead, my Father chose to write about the simple pleasure he and his war time buddy took from the different meals they shared while the war raged and Europe and North Africa were torn to shreds about them. I have not given the poem its proper title because it contains the name of that friend who, like my Father, long ago passed on, so cannot grant his permission to use it here. Instead I have taken for that purpose the penultimate line which I think is appropriate.

Our Monument? — Our Bully Tins

...Robert (Bob) William Scott *(Sergeant Major, Royal Artillery; and great Dad) 1914 - 1988*

Look back old Pal on days gone by!
Six years of war and all it brings.
We've been good mates have you and I.
Together seen our share of things

We've had our moments – good and bad –
In mud and ice and desert sands,
But pause a while and think, old lad,
Of meals we've shared in many lands.

Banana Splits in Capetown,
Sour lemons shared at Guaggi,
The mixed grills bought at Folkstone
And green limes at Deolali.

The dates devoured in Irak,
Tomatoes at Catania,
The tea we brewed at Mefrak,
And fried sole at Natanya.

Fruit salad from old Cairo,
The Camembert from France,
Cold Icecream at Reposto,
And cocoa near Arromanche.

No fame for us though Britain wins –
No cheers, no thanks, no flags unfurled.
Our monument? - Our bully tins
Lying scattered round half the world.

About the Author

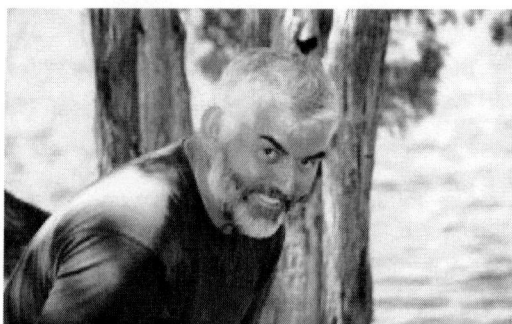

Born in England, raised on the banks of a river in the Sussex countryside, Jim Scott from a young age developed strong spiritual connections with the natural realm. He wasn't to understand this until much later in life when this realization explained the somewhat unique atavistic philosophies that evolved from his extensive travels and often ran against the grain of mainstream thinking.

Mostly working and often living in close proximity with nature he developed a profound respect for the balance of how life is lived according to the planet's natural wisdom. This is represented in his writing where he is not shy to criticize what he considers the synthetic, artificial worlds of cities, industry and reliance upon financial success, while advocating environmental causes, bucolic lifestyles and indigenous groups who yet follow the Old Ways of natural balance. Such views, backed by extensive and diverse experience within many realms of human existence and coupled with a keen interest in the written word created the perfect opportunity to express what he has seen and believes within his many fascinating stories, poems and essays.

The list of countries to which Jim has wandered is long: Morocco, Rhodesia/Zimbabwe, Peru, Gibraltar, India, Antigua, South Africa, Portugal, and many, many more where his sojourns were lengthy enough for adventures to be lived and insightful philosophies developed from them. It is from such experiences among such disparate cultures, landscapes, politics and economies that the stories and verses in his books were forged.

A father of three, Jim now lives in Canada and spends as much time as he can in the British Virgin Islands where two of his children were born and where, out of all the places to which he has wandered and in which he has sojourned, he feels most at home.

Other books in Jim Scott's
Wanderings and Sojourns series

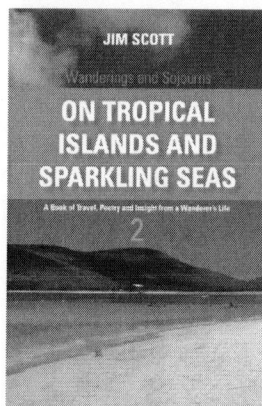

For more details about the books, the author, there is a website www.caridiangroup.com.

There is also a Facebook group page which can be found by searching on Facebook for **Wanderings and Sojourns**.